America's Rising
STAR CHEFS®

presents

CRÈME DE LA CRÈME

VOLUME III

FEATURING OVER 100 NEW RECIPES FROM AMERICA'S HOTTEST NEW CHEFS

WITH WINE PAIRINGS AND DECORATING TIPS

SANTA FE PUBLISHING

SAN FRANCISCO

PHOTOGRAPHER

WILLIAM McKELLAR

BOOK DESIGN

MICHELLE DUVAL

WRITER

ANTHONY STEPHEN TIANO

EDITORS

BETHANY JEAN CLEMENT

MATTHEW HUMPHREY

STYLIST

WILLIAM McKELLAR

STYLE SEGMENTS DESIGN

LOUISA CHENG

LISA FUCHSLIN

PATRICIA WILSON

INDEX/PRODUCTION ASSISTANT

EMILY LUNDBERG

EXECUTIVE CHEF

MARK TIANO

SOUS CHEF

SALENA SINCLAIR

PUBLISHER

ANTHONY TIANO

Copyright © 1996 by Santa Fe Publishing
877 Bryant Street, Suite 210
San Francisco, CA 94103
Tel: 415-575-1450   Fax: 415-575-1459

ISBN: 0-9641403-3-0
Library of Congress Catalog Card Number: 96-090614
Manufactured in Singapore

COVER:

Roy Breiman's medallions of lamb wrapped in red onions

CONTENTS

In 1993, after almost three decades of watching the steady flow of programs about cooking that had insinuated themselves into the public television weekend schedules and marveling at the different styles of cooking that are American Cuisine, I wondered what it would be like to meet some of the rising stars around the country and to share their personalities and special dishes with public television audiences.

What I found was surprising only for the depth of passion and commitment these remarkable young people bring to their craft and lives. They are universally bright and talented. While the food is as different as the many regions of America, the desire to be creative and the love of cooking is found in every chef.

"A good cook is like a sorcerer who dispenses happiness on a plate," says Bernard Guillas of the Marine Room at the La Jolla Beach and Tennis Club in southern California. The feeling of dispensing happiness is a common thread for our fifteen stars this year, from David Reardon at The Orchid in Hawaii, who prepared an absolutely wonderful free-range chicken dish and whose years with the Sheraton Hotel chain have allowed him to continually improve his cuisine and his creativity, to Elizabeth Terry of Savannah, Georgia, whose Elizabeth on 37th has become an institution of great food and southern hospitality.

Whether it is "food from the heart," as David Holben of Mediterraneo describes his cooking or RoxSand Scocos's efforts to fuse cuisines from around the world ("Perhaps fusion cuisine is the first step toward a cross-cultural Brave New World"), each of the chefs brought a distinct creativity

On location at Signature Properties' Trieste model home

and special personality to our kitchen. We were better for it.

This year we asked *Food Arts Magazine* to help us identify the hot new chefs for inclusion in our series. After meetings, faxes, phone calls and some substitutions (chefs do move around a lot), we identified fifteen people from around the country, with special emphasis on some of our great smaller cities: Milwaukee, San Diego, Minneapolis, Savannah, Durham and Phoenix. It is a great group and the food is both easy to prepare and delicious. I know because I tasted some of every dish!

Good food demands good beverages and we found someone to help us pair wine with the dishes prepared for the programs. Carolyn Wente, President of Wente Vineyards, gave us her Wine and Food 101 course and now we know almost as much as the waitstaff at our favorite restaurant.

Take these men and women and their cooking styles and passion, add an air of competence and some easy-to-follow directions, and you have the makings of a very special book. Please use this book regularly for all occasions from the everyday to the extra special.

Bon appetit.

— *Anthony Tiano*

ACKNOWLEDGEMENTS

In the third year of our *America's Rising Star Chefs* project, we are grateful for the support we have received from many people. Our third season has been particularly rewarding and we are delighted to share this effort with some old friends and to welcome some new ones to our family as well. Many people gave deeply of themselves to make this project happen. We express our deep appreciation to:

The editorial staff at *Food Arts Magazine, The Magazine for Professionals,* with particular thanks to Michael Batterberry, Founding Editor, for help in selecting our fifteen chefs for the year.

The ITT Sheraton Corporation for their support over the past three years; particularly to Stephen Powell, Vice President for Marketing.

The Brita Products Company of Oakland, California for their continued support.

Carolyn Wente, President of **Wente Vineyards** in Livermore, California, for help in pairing wines with the dishes and for providing solid and useful information about wine and food combinations for the television series and this book.

Mike Ghielmetti of **Signature Properties** of Pleasanton, California, for allowing us to move our army of technicians, chefs, kitchen help, photographers, writers, and decorators into their Trieste model home for two weeks.

Cost Plus World Market and Christine Hildebrand for supplying a unique and broad selection of furniture, collectibles, and tableware which allowed us to create innovative style segments, and for assistance in writing those sections of the book and television programs.

Draeger's Supermarkets, Inc. and Tony Draeger in Menlo Park, California, for their help in providing the highest quality ingredients for the project and for keeping the crew well fed.

The staff at the **Sheraton Four Points Hotel** in Pleasanton, California, who accommodated our every need.

Diablo Valley College Hotel & Restaurant Management Program for a great group of young prep chefs and interns.

Alden Lane Nursery for flowers and plants.

Aveda for makeup, hair products, and artists.

Chefwear USA, Inc. for gifts to make our chefs feel at home.

Miraglia Catering and Event Planning for prep kitchen shelves and grills.

Napa Valley Kitchens for ingredients and chef gifts.

RevereWare and their Solutions line of cookware.

Roscan for kitchen utensils.

Sunbeam Household Products for kitchen appliances.

Sur La Table for kitchen utensils and equipment.

Underwood Ranches for vegetables.

Please refer to the resource list for contact information on these great friends of ours.

Thanks to the Santa Fe Ventures staff including Sharron Ames, Louisa Cheng, Lisa Fuchslin, Danielle Greenwood, Lennlee Melton, David Myer, and Patricia Wilson who worked so hard to make this project happen. Special thanks to my family who pitched in when it was needed, and especially to my son Steve for doing everything from driving the truck to writing this book.

ALDEN LANE NURSERY
981 Alden Lane
Livermore, CA 94550
(510) 447-0280 F(510) 443-8512

AVEDA W.D.G./WEST, INC.
856 Mitten Road
Burlingame, CA 94010
(415) 697-5656 F(415) 697-5173
In California 1(800) 822-8332

THE BRITA PRODUCTS COMPANY
1221 Broadway
Oakland, CA 94612-1888
(510) 271-7000 F(510) 208-1575

CHEFWEAR, INC.
833 North Orleans, Fourth Floor
Chicago, IL 60610-3049
(800) 568-2433 F(312) 654-2209

CORNING/REVERE
CONSUMER INFORMATION CENTER
P.O. Box 1994
Waynesboro, VA 22980
(800) 999-3436 F(540) 949-9118

COST PLUS WORLD MARKET
201 Clay Street
Oakland, CA 94607
(510) 893-7300 F(510) 465-6805

DIABLO VALLEY COLLEGE
HOTEL & RESTAURANT
MANAGEMENT PROGRAM
321 Golf Club Road
Pleasant Hill, CA 94523
(510) 685-1230 F(510)687-6384

DRAEGER'S SUPERMARKETS, INC.
1010 University Drive
Menlo Park, CA 94026-6203
(415) 688-0688 F(415) 326-3718

FOOD ARTS MAGAZINE
387 Park Avenue South
New York, NY 10016
(212) 684-4224 F(212) 684-5424

ITT SHERATON CORPORATION
60 State Street, Boston, MA 02109
(617) 367-3600
F(617) 367-5500 (Marketing)
(800) 325-3535 (Reservations)

MIRAGLIA CATERING
& EVENT PLANNING
2094 Burroughs Avenue
San Leandro, CA 94577
(510)483-5210 F(510) 483-6855

NAPA VALLEY KITCHENS
4 Financial Plaza, Napa, CA 94558
(707) 254-3700 F(707) 259-0219

ROSCAN/G. ROSENTHAL
IMPORTS LTD.
5850 Thimens
Saint Laurent, Québec
Canada H4S IS5
(514) 335-4348 F(514) 335-4349

SIGNATURE PROPERTIES
6612 Owens Drive
Pleasanton, CA 94588
(510) 463-1122 F(510) 417-5815

SUNBEAM HOUSEHOLD PRODUCTS
P.O. Box 1964 Laurel, MS 39441
1(800) 528-7713 F(601) 425-7877

SUR LA TABLE CATALOG DIVISION
410 Terry Avenue North
Seattle, WA 98109-5229
(800) 243-0852
F(206) 682-1026

UNDERWOOD RANCHES
P.O. Box 607, Somis, CA 93066
(800) 447-7746
F(805) 386- 4389
E-mail: undrwood@west.net

UNIVERSITY OF CALIFORNIA, DAVIS
DEPARTMENT OF VITICULTURE
& ENOLOGY
Davis, CA 95616-8749
(916) 752-0387 F(916)752-0382
Internet: www.wineserver.ucdavis.edu
E-mail: acnoble@ucdavis.edu

WENTE VINEYARDS
5565 Tesla Road
Livermore, CA 94550
(510) 447-3603 F(510) 447-4837

BEN BARKER

MAGNOLIA GRILL
DURHAM, NORTH CAROLINA

APPETIZERS

MARINATED RED AND YELLOW
TOMATOES WITH FIELD PEAS
VINAIGRETTE AND HERBED
CHÈVRE

SUMMER SHELL BEAN
MINESTRE WITH TOMATO
BRUSCHETTA

ENTRÉES

GRILLED GEORGIA QUAIL ON
ROASTED BUTTERNUT RISOTTO
WITH SUN-DRIED CHERRIES
AND MAPLE GLAZE

SPICY GRILLED SHRIMP AND
GRITS CAKES, COUNTRY HAM,
AND "REDEYE" VINAIGRETTE

DESSERT

BERGY BUTTERMILK
CHEESECAKE

"Folks would bring their pride-and-joys, their signature dishes, to family reunions, summertime barbecues, and church suppers," recalls Chef Ben Barker of growing up in Chapel Hill, North Carolina. "As a child, you'd listen to the adults and learn what was special. Typically, you'd go through and take some of all the main courses, the side dishes, and condiments. But, if someone's dessert was particularly fine, you'd run over and snatch that first." Those family picnics and summertime affairs still color his cooking style today. "I chose to cook the flavors I know in a modern way."

A graduate of the Culinary Institute of America in New York, Chef Barker met his wife/partner and gifted pastry chef, Karen, on their first day of classes. After graduation they moved back to the Durham-Chapel Hill area and worked at La Rèsidence in Chapel Hill, then at the Fearrington House restaurant in Pittsboro where Chef Barker initiated the "Cuisine of the New South" as a theme.

In 1986, Ben and Karen converted a Durham neighborhood grocery store into the Magnolia, where the motto "Not Afraid of Flavor" has inspired a regionally-based seasonal cuisine. Ben and Karen serve only the freshest of ingredients in season: "We often serve food harvested the same day, and that 'straight from the garden to table flavor' has a direct impact on the finished plate."

Chef Barker's awards include being listed in *Food & Wine*'s "Who's Who of Southern Cooking" in 1988. In 1992, he was named one of *Esquire*'s "Rising Star Chefs." *Food & Wine* again recognized Barker in 1993, as one of the "Ten Best New Chefs in America."

In 1995, the Barkers opened their second restaurant, POP's, a trattoria, also located in Durham.

PHOTO: *Marinated red and yellow tomatoes with field peas vinaigrette and herbed chèvre.*

BEN BARKER

MARINATED RED AND YELLOW TOMATOES WITH FIELD PEAS VINAIGRETTE AND HERBED CHÈVRE

(Serves 8)

HERBED CHÈVRE (GOAT CHEESE)

1   lb. fresh chèvre, sliced into 8 disks
2   Tbs. Italian parsley, chopped fine
2   Tbs. fresh basil, chopped
3   cloves garlic, smashed
10 grinds fresh black pepper
1   lemon, zested or grated
4   oz. olive oil

Make sure all the ingredients are room temperature. In a bowl combine the herbs, garlic, black pepper, lemon zest, and olive oil. Whisk to combine the ingredients. Marinate sliced chèvre in olive oil mixture for 6 hours or up to 2 days.

TOMATOES

2   lbs. dead-ripe red and yellow tomatoes, cored and sliced ¹/₂-inch thick
2   Tbs. Italian parsley, chopped
2   Tbs. fresh basil, chopped
¹/₂ cup basil-infused Consorzio olive oil
    Freshly ground black pepper
    Splash red wine vinegar
    Basil leaves to garnish

Combine marinade ingredients. Dip tomatoes in marinade and place flat on a plate. Keep covered for up to 3 hours.

VINAIGRETTE FOR PEAS

2   oz. cider vinegar
4   oz. virgin peanut oil or olive oil
2   Tbs. Italian parsley, chopped
2   Tbs. fresh basil, chopped
    Salt and freshly ground pepper to taste

Combine vinaigrette ingredients in large bowl. Set over an ice bath and set aside.

PEAS

1   qt. shelled, fresh purple hull, blackeye, or field peas (or substitute frozen peas)
¹/₄ cup peanut or safflower oil
5   oz. onion, finely diced
1   med. carrot, finely diced
2   stalks celery, finely diced
1   sm. green pepper, finely diced
1   sm. red pepper, finely diced
1   bay leaf, preferably fresh
1   Tbs. garlic, minced
1   pinch red pepper flake
3   cups vegetable or chicken stock or water
1¹/₂ tsp. salt
    Scallions, thinly sliced on the diagonal for garnish
    Salt and pepper to taste

In a heavy-bottomed pan, cook onion and celery in peanut oil over moderate heat until soft. Add peppers, bay leaf, garlic, and pepper flake and cook for 1 minute. Add peas, stock (or water) and bring to boil. Reduce to simmer. Cook until peas are tender. Add 1¹/₂ teaspoons of salt to vinaigrette in bowl, stock and all. Toss until cool; season with salt and pepper to taste.

To Serve

Arrange 4 tomatoes on a serving platter. Top with field peas vinaigrette and herbed chèvre, sprinkle with scallions, and drizzle with basil-infused olive oil. Serve at room temperature.

SUMMER SHELL BEAN MINESTRE WITH TOMATO BRUSCHETTA

(serves 8)

VEGETABLE STOCK

3   leeks, trimmed, washed, and sliced crosswise
6   oz. carrots, peeled and sliced thin
2   ribs of celery, diced

4   oz. onion, peeled and sliced

12   oz. very ripe tomatoes, cored and rough-chopped

4   corn cobs (4 whole ears, silver queen preferred, shucked, kernels cut, cobs scraped, and kernels plus cob scrapings set aside and reserved for minestre)

6   whole black peppercorns

2   cloves garlic, mashed

$1/2$ tsp. crushed red pepper flake

6   parsley sprigs

4   fresh thyme sprigs

2   bay leaves

6   cups cold water

Combine all ingredients in a large pot. Bring to a boil and simmer for 30 minutes. Strain the vegetable stock and set aside to cool. The stock should be refrigerated if it will not be used immediately.

TOMATO BRUSCHETTA

8   slices semolina baguette, grilled or toasted, rubbed with garlic and olive oil

3–4   dead-ripe tomatoes, peeled, seeded, and chopped

2   Tbs. basil, chopped

Salt, pepper, and olive oil to taste

Combine tomatoes, salt, pepper, and olive oil. Spread on toast.

SHELL BEAN MINESTRE

1   bay leaf

4   Tbs. olive oil

2   leeks, trimmed, quartered, cleaned, and sliced crosswise

4   oz. onion, diced

3   oz. fennel bulb, diced

4   oz. red pepper, diced

2   Tbs. garlic, minced

$1/2$ tsp. fennel seed, crushed

$1/4$ tsp. red pepper flake

2   cups fresh tiny lima beans

1   cup fresh field peas or black-eyed peas

4   cups vegetable stock

8   oz. fresh chanterelles or shiitakes, trimmed and sliced

RESERVED CORN KERNELS (SEE ABOVE VEGETABLE STOCK RECIPE)

1   cup tomato concasse

$1/2$ cup flat leaf parsley, chopped

$1/2$ cup fresh basil leaves, chopped

Salt and black pepper to taste

SHAVED SONOMA DRY JACK CHEESE

In a nonreactive, heavy-bottomed saucepan, heat olive oil over medium heat. Add bay leaf, leeks, onion, fennel, and pepper. Cook covered over low heat until softened. Raise heat to medium and stir in garlic, fennel seed, and red pepper flake. Cook for 1 minute. Add limas, field peas, and 4 cups of vegetable stock. Bring to a boil, skim, and reduce to simmer. Cook 8 to 20 minutes or until beans are tender. While beans are cooking, sauté mushrooms in olive oil until crisp and cooked through. Reserve. When beans are done, stir in the corn and mushrooms and simmer 3 to 4 minutes. Season generously with salt and black pepper. This portion may be prepared ahead of time.

To Serve

Heat minestre over medium heat (add more vegetable stock if too thick). Stir in tomato concasse and herbs. Check seasoning for desired taste. Ladle into bowls, garnish with shaved cheese, and serve with tomato bruschetta.

SPICY GRILLED SHRIMP AND GRITS CAKES, COUNTRY HAM AND "REDEYE" VINAIGRETTE
(Serves 6)

SHRIMP

$1^1/4$ lbs. 15 to 20 count large shrimp, peeled and deveined, shells reserved

1   tsp. cracked fennel seed

1   tsp. crushed red pepper flakes

6   cloves garlic, peeled and mashed

1   tsp. freshly ground black pepper

$^1/_3$ cup cold-pressed peanut oil (or olive oil)

12   6-inch wooden skewers, soaked in cold water

Zest of 1 lemon, minced

Divide the shrimp into 6 equal portions and, using 2 skewers per portion, skewer the shrimp through the heads with one skewer and the tails with the other skewer so the shrimp are equidistant on them, thus facilitating turning them on the grill. Combine the fennel seed, lemon zest, red pepper flakes, garlic, black pepper, and oil and thoroughly coat the skewered shrimp. Refrigerate and marinate for 2 to 4 hours.

SHRIMP OIL

1   tsp. tomato paste

1   cup cold-pressed peanut oil (or olive oil)

Reserved shrimp shells

Heat 2 tablespoons peanut oil until shimmering. Stir in reserved shrimp shells and cook 2 minutes. Stir in tomato paste, add remaining oil, and heat to a bare simmer. Remove from heat and steep for 2 hours. Pour the shrimp oil through a cheesecloth-lined strainer or chinois into a bowl, pressing on the shells to extract all the liquid. If using a charcoal grill, start fire now.

VINAIGRETTE

1   Tbs. cold-pressed peanut oil (or olive oil)

4   oz. thinly sliced country ham, trimmed of all fat, julienned

3   Tbs. brewed strong black coffee

$^1/_2$ cup balsamic vinegar

1   cup fresh homemade chicken stock

4   cloves garlic, peeled and finely minced

$^1/_2$ tsp. crushed red pepper flakes

2   Tbs. fresh thyme leaves

$^1/_2$ lb. mesclun, or mixed young peppery greens, washed and dried

Salt to taste

Heat the tablespoon of oil in an 8-inch sauté pan over medium-high heat. Add the country ham julienne and sauté until lightly browned and crisp. Remove from pan, drain, pat dry, and reserve. Pour off the remaining fat and deglaze pan with the black coffee. Add the balsamic vinegar, bring to a boil, and reduce by half. Add the chicken stock, return to a boil, and reduce by 2/3. Remove from heat, stir in the garlic and red pepper flakes, and allow to cool. Strain. Whisk in the shrimp oil and thyme, and season with salt. Reserve at room temperature. Wash and dry the mesclun and reserve in the refrigerator.

GRITS CAKES

1   qt. chicken stock

1   Tbs. salt

1   cup stone-ground yellow grits

2   lg. eggs

4   egg yolks

1   cup Parmesan or Sonoma Dry jack cheese, grated

2   tablespoons unsalted butter

Salt, freshly ground black pepper, and Tabasco to taste

Thyme sprays to garnish

Preheat the oven to 350°F. Generously butter an 8" x 11" pan (or jellyroll pan; the dimensions will determine thickness of grits cakes). Over high heat bring the chicken stock to boil in a 2- or 3-quart saucepan. Reduce to medium-high heat and add the salt and grits, stirring continuously for 5 minutes or until grits have thickened. Be careful; spattering grits can burn! Whisk the eggs and yolks in a bowl, carefully adding a small amount of thickened grits. Then whisk the egg and grit mixture into the remaining grits until well combined. Mix in the cheese and season to taste with the salt, black pepper, and Tabasco. Pour into the buttered baking pan and bake for 25 to 30 minutes until the mixture is well set (it will be firm and have a lightly mottled surface). Cool and refrigerate.

To Serve

Using a 3-inch biscuit cutter, cut the chilled grits cakes into 6 rounds. (The scraps make nice snacks when baked in a hot oven and tossed with sautéed mushrooms.) Preheat the oven to

400°F. Reheat the grits on a cookie sheet or a nonstick pan in the oven. Toss the country ham and greens with the vinaigrette. Grill or broil the shrimp, turning once, and cook them until just opaque. Season with salt and remove them from the skewers. Place the grits cakes on warm plates, top them with the dressed greens, and place the grilled shrimp on the greens with their tails pointing up. Drizzle the remaining vinaigrette around the perimeter of the plate (to resemble a "broken" vinaigrette, or "redeye gravy"). Garnish with thyme sprays.

Wine Recommendation:
Ivan Tamas Pinot Grigio

GRILLED GEORGIA QUAIL ON ROASTED BUTTERNUT RISOTTO WITH SUN-DRIED CHERRIES AND MAPLE GLAZE

(Serves 8)

8   semi-boneless fresh quail, 4 to 5 ounces each, or frozen
    quail which have been defrosted 24 hours in refrigerator

Trim wing tips from quail and reserve. Make an incision in skin at the base of breast bone and insert legs through incision. Quail will look like a frog you ran over in the driveway.

QUAIL MARINADE
1   Tbs. maple syrup
2   Tbs. bourbon
2   shallots, peeled and sliced thin
1   Tbs. fresh thyme leaves
1   tsp. coarsely ground black pepper
2   oz. peanut or other mild oil

Stir maple syrup and bourbon together; add in remaining ingredients. Divide marinade among quail and refrigerate, turning occasionally, for 4 hours or overnight. Remove quail from refrigeration at least 30 minutes before cooking.

MAPLE GLAZE
    Reserved quail wing tips
2   oz. sun-dried cherries

PHOTO: *Spicy grilled shrimp and grits cakes, country ham and "redeye" vinaigrette*

$^1/_2$ cup bourbon
1   Tbs. peanut oil
1   shallot, minced
2   cloves of garlic, minced
3   Tbs. maple syrup
2   Tbs. cider vinegar
$1^1/_2$ qts. homemade chicken stock
2   lg. sprigs fresh thyme
    Salt and freshly ground black pepper to taste

In a small saucepan, heat bourbon with sun-dried cherries. Remove from heat and set aside to cool. Strain and reserve bourbon and cherries. In a heavy-bottomed saucepan, heat oil over medium heat until simmering. Add wing tips and cook over medium heat until brown and crispy. Add shallots and garlic; cook for 1 minute. Add maple syrup, reserved bourbon, and vinegar; bring to boil, reduce heat, and simmer until reduced by half. Add chicken stock, bring to boil, and reduce heat to medium. Simmer, skimming as needed, until reduced to approximately 1 1/2 cups. Add thyme sprigs and remove from heat to infuse for 10 minutes. Strain. Adjust seasoning with salt and freshly ground black pepper. Add reserved cherries and keep warm or reheat before serving.

ROASTED BUTTERNUT SQUASH PUREE

1   small butternut squash
3   Tbs. peanut oil

Peel and cut the butternut squash into 2 parts. Use the neck of the squash for the risotto; cut into a fine dice. Cut the remaining portion into 1-inch chunks, toss with peanut oil, and roast at 350°F until soft (approximately 20 to 30 minutes). Purée in a food processor or through food mill. Reserve.

WINE

The Grape's the Thing

The most important element in making wine is starting with one-hundred-percent-natural grape juice. Growing good grapes is critical to everything that happens in making wine. If you don't have good grapes, you'll never make great wine. As the grape ripens, the sugar content increases and the acid content decreases. Grapes are picked when there is a nice balance between sugar and acid. The wine maker's job is to take the farmer's grapes and nurture them through the wine making process.

In selecting wines to go with a meal, go from lighter to heavier. A light white wine will go well with the tomato salad, and a heavier, sweeter wine will go well with the spicy shrimp.

ROASTED BUTTERNUT RISOTTO

2   oz. clarified butter or peanut oil
1/2 cup onion, finely diced
1   cup butternut squash, peeled, finely diced
1/2 cup fennel bulb (or celery), finely diced
1   Tbs. garlic, minced
2   whole cloves
12   oz. Arborio rice
6   oz. white wine
1   qt. homemade chicken stock, simmering (or more, as needed)
1/4 cup roasted butternut squash purée
1   Tbs. fresh thyme leaves
3   Tbs. unsalted butter, cut into three pieces
2   Tbs. freshly grated Parmesan or Sonoma Dry jack
Salt and pepper to taste

In a heavy-bottomed pan, heat clarified butter or oil over medium heat. Add onion, butternut squash, and fennel, and cook until softened but not colored. Add garlic, cloves, and rice, and cook 2 to 3 minutes until rice is translucent. Add white wine and cook until mostly absorbed. Add 6 ounces chicken stock and cook until mostly absorbed. Repeat stock additions until rice is cooked 80% through (cut a kernel in half; it will have a fine pinhead of raw center). Pour rice onto a sheetpan, spread, and set aside to cool. This portion may be prepared ahead of time and refrigerated once cooled. Be sure to remove cloves. To finish rice: heat over medium heat with 6 ounces chicken stock absorbed. Stir in purée, unsalted butter, thyme, and cheese. Adjust seasoning.

To Serve
Light the charcoal grill or preheat the broiler. Remove quail from marinade, wipe off excess marinade, and season generously with salt and pepper. Heat sauce and finish risotto; keep warm. Grill quail, breast-side down, on grill (or breast-side up under a broiler). Turn the quail 45 degrees (for cool-looking grill marks) after 2 minutes; cook for 2 minutes longer. Turn quail over and cook for 3 minutes longer until breast is springy and legs are done. Divide risotto among 8 warm plates and top

each with one quail. Spoon a scant 1 ounce of sauce over each, scattering cherries around. Garnish with thyme sprig and serve immediately.

BERGY BUTTERMILK CHEESECAKE
(One 10-inch cake)

CRUST

   1$^1/_2$ cups graham cracker crumbs

   $^1/_2$ cup yellow cornmeal

   2   Tbs. sugar

   3   oz. butter, melted

Preheat oven to 350°F. Butter a 10-inch springform pan. In a medium-sized bowl, combine graham cracker crumbs, cornmeal, sugar, and melted butter. Press mixture into bottom and up approximately 1 inch on the sides of the pan. Bake at 350°F until lightly golden (approximately 10 minutes). Remove from the oven and reserve.

CHEESECAKE BATTER

   4   oz. butter, room temperature

   1$^1/_2$ lbs. cream cheese, room temperature

   2   lemons, zested or grated

   1   cup sugar

   $^3/_4$ cup buttermilk

   1   tsp. vanilla

   4   eggs

Cream room temperature butter and cream cheese with lemon zest and sugar until smooth. Add buttermilk and vanilla. Beat, scraping the sides of the bowl occasionally until well combined. Add eggs and slowly beat just to combine. Do not over mix. Pour into reserved crust. Bake 25 minutes at 350°F. Turn oven to 300°F and bake an additional 25 minutes. Turn oven to low setting and bake until done (approximately 20 minutes; cake will be set around the edges and barely jiggly in the very center). Cool and chill several hours before serving. Serve with a mixture of seasonal fresh berries.

STYLE

Magnolias and Good Friends

Transplanting the hospitality and leisure of the South to your friends and family requires a bit of imagination and some simple materials for your table.

Place mats taped together make a beautiful table runner and white plates allow subtle colors on the table to shine. The plates are topped by luxurious double-folded napkins in white bow napkin rings that match each place setting.

Candles and flowers floating in a clear glass bowl allow the table to remain festive without the heaviness of a large centerpiece. Lightly tinted stemware in green or blue completes the setting.

A poet said, "The South is a state of mind," and you will have a sure hit with this Southern *Rising Star* setting.

ROY BREIMAN

THE RESTAURANT AT MEADOWOOD
ST. HELENA, CALIFORNIA

APPETIZER

GRILLED CAESAR SALAD WITH
FOCACCIA CROUTONS AND
REGGIANO

ENTRÉES

MEDALLIONS OF LAMB
WRAPPED IN RED ONIONS

ROASTED BABY PHEASANT WITH
APRICOT, LEMONGRASS, CINNA-
MON AND CLOVES

MEDALLIONS OF LOBSTER WITH
BABY GREEN PEAS AND TRUF-
FLED MACARONI

DESSERT

MILLEFEUILLE OF CARAMELIZED
BANANAS, BLACK CURRANTS,
AND CHOCOLATE CHIPS SERVED
WITH A CARAMEL SAUCE

"I think it's absolutely vital that you learn the correct way to cook. Your final signature style will grow out of all the accumulated best you've learned from others along the way," says Chef de Cuisine Roy Breiman of the acclaimed Restaurant at Meadowood Resort in Napa Valley.

A California native, Breiman began his culinary career at the age of sixteen washing dishes. Realizing his love for the culinary arts, Chef Breiman entered a six-month school program run by Gérard Collet, a French chef and instructor at Le Cordon Rouge. It was here that Breiman was first introduced to French cuisine. Unable to afford the nearly $4,000 tuition, Breiman worked for Collet at Le Cordon Rouge as a *stagaire* in exchange. "I soon found out *stagaire* means a gofer assistant to the chef," recalls Breiman.

After graduation, Breiman worked in the kitchens of Ernie's in San Francisco and Le Meridien Hotel's restaurants, Maurice in New York and Antoine in Newport Beach, California. But Chef Breiman attributes much of his style and creativity to the training he received in the South of France. He worked under Bruno Cirino at Le Chateau Eza overlooking the Mediterranean and Dominique Le Stanc at the Hotel Negresco in Nice. It was Le Stanc that instilled in Breiman the importance of a healthy mind, body, and spirit.

In Breiman's two and a half years at Meadowood, he has brought acclaim to the Restaurant with his cooking techniques and the freshest of local ingredients. *Country Inns* magazine awarded Meadowood the "Best Inn Dining" prize, and *Wine Spectator* gave it an Award of Honor. Critic Dan Fendle says of Breiman's menu: "Every meal at Meadowood is a kind of 'present' that you unwrap course by course."

PHOTO: *Grilled Caesar salad with focaccia croutons and reggiano*

GRILLED CAESAR SALAD WITH FOCACCIA CROUTONS AND REGGIANO

(Serves 6)

GARLIC OIL

$1/4$ cup olive oil

2 whole cloves garlic

Combine $1/4$ cup olive oil with 2 cloves chopped garlic in a small pan. Slowly bring to a boil. Remove from heat. Let rest 30 minutes.

ROMAINE

6 tight hearts of Romaine (core attached)

3 Tbs. garlic oil

Salt and pepper to taste

Rinse and dry romaine. Slice each heart in half and brush with garlic olive oil. Season with salt and pepper. Set aside for grilling.

FOCACCIA CROUTONS

1 lb. focaccia bread

3 Tbs. garlic oil

Brush Focaccia with garlic oil. Grill 30 seconds on each side. Cut into triangles 1 inch in diameter. Set aside for final presentation.

CAESAR DRESSING

$1^1/2$ cups olive oil

$1/2$ tsp. Tabasco

3 oz. Reggiano ($1^1/2$ oz. grated, $1^1/2$ shaved)

1 Tbs. Worcestershire sauce

1 Tbs. white wine vinegar

1 Tbs. red wine vinegar

2 Tbs. balsamic vinegar

1 Tbs. black pepper

1 egg

4 cloves garlic, chopped

6 anchovies

$1/2$ lemon

Salt to taste

Combine all ingredients except olive oil into a food processor. Process ingredients until well mixed. Slowly combine olive oil until emulsified. Season with salt and set aside for final presentation.

To Serve

Preheat grill to high heat. Grill romaine approximately 5 to 10 seconds on each side. On a 12-inch serving plate, place 3 to 4 croutons in the center. Atop croutons place grilled romaine. Spoon 3 to 4 tablespoons of the Caesar dressing over the romaine. Garnish with shaved Reggiano and serve immediately.

MEDALLIONS OF LAMB WRAPPED IN RED ONION

(Serves 4)

LAMB STOCK

(The lamb stock should be prepared at least 1 day in advance.)

1 $3^1/2$ lb. saddle of lamb, bones only, chopped into 2 pieces (meat is used later in the recipe)

2 qts. water

1 qt. chicken stock

2 heads garlic, sliced in half horizontally

2 bunches thyme

2 bay leaves

Preheat the oven to 500°F and roast the lamb bones in a roasting pan until they are dark brown. Remove the bones from the oven and drain off the fat. Place the bones, water, chicken stock, garlic, thyme, and bay leaves into a large pot and cook over low heat for 4 hours, adding water whenever needed. Strain the mixture and refrigerate. The fat will solidify and should be removed and discarded.

LAMB MEDALLIONS

- 1   3$^1/_2$ lb. saddle of lamb (2 loins and 2 tenderloins)
- 1   potato
- 5   Roma tomatoes
- 3   red onions, peeled
- $^1/_2$ cup red wine vinegar
- 1   green zucchini
- 2   leaves brick pastry (or phyllo dough)
- 1   egg mixed with 2 Tbs. water, for egg wash
- 3–4 Tbs. olive oil
- $^1/_2$ bunch of fresh oregano, leaves only
- 2   cups Lamb Stock
- 12   fresh basil leaves

Salt and freshly ground black pepper to taste

Chervil or parsley sprigs (for garnish)

Place the tenderloins between sheets of plastic wrap and flatten until they are approximately 1/4 inch thick. Refrigerate the meat while preparing the vegetables.

Peel and cut the potato lengthwise into pieces 2 inches long and 1 inch wide. Cut these pieces into medallions. Place in a bowl of cold water and set aside. Blanch tomatoes in rapidly boiling water for 10 seconds. Remove from water and place in an ice bath to stop the cooking process. Peel the tomatoes, cut into squares, and remove the seeds. Cut the onions in half horizontally. Separate the outer $^2/_3$ of each half into individual layers and set them aside; reserve the centers. In a small pot, cook the outer layers of the onions in salted boiling water with the vinegar until they are tender, approximately 15 to 20

PHOTO: *Medallions of lamb wrapped in red onion*

minutes. Peel the zucchini carefully, slice the peel thinly, and discard the remainder or reserve it for another use.

Place 1 of the lamb tenderloins on a flat surface. On top of the meat, arrange 3 tomato quarters down the center and top them with some of the julienne zucchini peel. Season with salt and pepper. Roll the lamb to its original shape and place it on a leaf of pastry. Roll the tenderloin up in the pastry as you would an egg roll and seal the edges with some of the egg wash. Repeat the procedure with the second tenderloin. Cover and refrigerate the rolls.

Season the loins with salt and pepper and cook them in a sauté pan in olive oil over medium-high heat until they are medium rare (approximately 8 minutes) and reserve. Cook the pastry-wrapped tenderloins in a sauté pan in olive oil over medium heat until they are golden brown all over (approximately 3 minutes). Remove from heat and let rest for 2 to 3 minutes.

GARNISH

To make the garnish, thinly slice the reserved onion centers. Heat a little of the olive oil in a sauté pan and add the potatoes, onion slices, and oregano. Cook over medium heat until the vegetables are brown. Add the lamb stock to pan; continue cooking gently for 5 minutes. Just before serving, add the remaining tomato quarters, the basil leaves, and the outer layers of onion, and cook the mixture for 1 to 2 minutes until all the flavors are blended.

To Serve

Slice each lamb loin into 6 medallions, placing 3 in a triangle on each plate. Arrange the garnish in layers on the medallions: 1 piece of potato, 1 tomato quarter, 1 basil leaf, and, on top, 1 piece of onion. Cut each of the pastry-wrapped tenderloins into 6 1-inch slices and arrange 3 in a triangle on each plate.

Sauce the lamb with the stock that remains in the pan. Garnish with chervil, fresh fennel, and society garlic flowers. Serve immediately.

ROASTED BABY PHEASANT WITH APRICOT, LEMONGRASS, CINNAMON, AND CLOVES
(Serves 4)

PHEASANT

4	baby pheasants
2	Tbs. olive oil

Remove breast and legs from each pheasant. Place in refrigerator and reserve carcass for sauce. Place 2 tablespoons olive oil in a sauté pan. Cook over medium heat, placing pheasant skin side down, browning approximately 3 minutes on each side. Remove breast and cook legs an additional 2 minutes in a 425°F oven. Remove from oven and reserve for service.

PHEASANT SAUCE

	Pheasant carcasses
3	Tbs. butter
2	oz. ginger, peeled and sliced
1	cinnamon stick
2	sprigs lemongrass, sliced
12	cloves
2	cups white wine
1	lt. veal stock

Chop the carcass of each pheasant into 4 pieces. Place in a saucepan with 1 tablespoon of butter. Cook until golden brown. Add ginger, cinnamon, sliced lemongrass, and cloves. Deglaze caramelized sauce with white wine. Reduce until almost dry. Add veal stock and reduce by 3/4. Strain mixture and bring sauce back to a boil. Add 2 tablespoons butter. Mix thoroughly. Set aside, keeping warm. Just before service, return sauce to heat and bring to a boil.

APRICOT SAUCE

$1/2$ cup butter

4 Tbs. sugar

10 oz. dried apricots (cut in quarters)

4 Tbs. black currants

2 limes, zested

1 Tbs. lemongrass, finely chopped

Chervil (for garnish)

In a saucepan, add remaining butter, sugar, apricots, black currants, lime zest, and 1 tablespoon chopped lemongrass. Cook over low heat until well incorporated. Set aside. Keep warm.

To Serve

In the center of the plate, place a circle of 5 tablespoons of the apricot mixture. Lay the pheasant breasts and legs on top of apricot mixture. Pour approximately 5 tablespoons boiling sauce over each plate. Garnish with chervil (optional). Serve immediately.

MEDALLIONS OF LOBSTER WITH BABY GREEN PEAS AND TRUFFLED MACARONI

(Serves 4)

LOBSTER

4 lobsters ($1^1/_4$ lbs. in size)

2 lbs. fresh green peas, removed from pods

$1/2$ lb. dried Italian macaroni

1 sprig of basil (for garnish)

Boil lobsters for approximately $4^1/_2$ minutes. Remove from liquid and set aside until cool. Remove meat from lobsters, reserve carcasses, and cut tail meat into medallions. Refrigerate. Save lobster carcass for sauce. Cook macaroni in salted boiling water until fully cooked. Cook green peas in salted boiling water until fully cooked.

WINE

America's French Wine Heritage

Many of the grape varieties planted in America originated in France. Chardonnay and Sauvignon Blanc were brought over from the Burgundy and the Bordeau regions of France as were our predominant reds, Cabernet Sauvignon and Merlot. We have essentially the same grapes in America as in France but they are planted in different soils and climates which result in different flavors. For example, California red wines have a more intense fruit character than their French counterparts.

Tannins are found in all wines but are more dominant in red wines. In making red wine, the skins are left on the grapes to add color. With the color comes the tannin. An acid, tannin helps cut through the oiliness of red meat to bring out the flavor of a meal.

LOBSTER SAUCE

lobster carcasses

$1/2$ Tbs. olive oil

2 carrots, chopped

2 onions, chopped

1 head garlic, cut in half

$1/2$ bunch thyme

1 Tbs. tomato paste or fresh tomato

1 cup white wine

2 Tbs. butter

$1/4$ cup heavy cream (optional)

2 bay leaves

Brown lobster carcasses in a sauce pot with $1/2$ tablespoon olive oil. Add carrots, onion, garlic, thyme, tomato paste, and bay leaves. Deglaze with white wine. Simmer on low heat for approximately 5 minutes or until reduced by half. Add enough water to cover carcasses and cook slowly for 45 to 60 minutes. Strain, saving sauce. Place sauce into small sauce pot and bring to a boil. Incorporate butter and cream into sauce. Place sauce into blender and liquefy. Set aside.

TRUFFLED MACARONI

$1/2$ cup beef bouillon or veal stock

$1/2$ lb. cooked Italian macaroni

$1/2$ truffle, sliced thin

$1/4$ cup shaved Parmigiana

In a heavy-bottomed sauce pot, reduce veal stock by one half and add macaroni with sliced truffle and shaved Parmigiana. Remove from heat.

To Serve

Brush lobster with olive oil and salt to taste. Reheat lobster in 475°F oven for approximately 2 minutes. Place medallions in half circle with claws at top of plate. Place macaroni between the claws and add a bit more of shaved Parmigiana and sliced truffle on top. Sauté green peas in a little butter and place peas along the outside of the lobster medallions. Spoon sauce over medallions and claws. Garnish with a sprig of basil. Serve immediately.

MILLEFEUILLE OF CARAMELIZED BANANAS, BLACK CURRANTS AND CHOCOLATE CHIPS SERVED WITH A CARAMEL SAUCE

(Serves 4)

PHYLLO LEAVES

6 leaves phyllo sheets (for layers)

6 oz. clarified butter

2 oz. sugar

To make the clarified butter, place 6 ounces butter into small saucepan and bring to a boil. Turn down heat and continue to cook, skimming the fat off the top until butter is clear yellow (approximately 20 minutes). Brush each layer of phyllo thoroughly with clarified butter and sprinkle granulated sugar evenly on each layer, stacking one on top of another. Continue this process until all layers are completed. Cut into 3-inch squares. Lay phyllo squares, slightly separated, between two pieces of parchment paper and place on a sheet tray. Lay another sheet tray on top. Cook in 375°F oven until golden brown (approximately 15 minutes). Remove from oven. Let cool. Remove from sheet tray and set aside.

CARAMEL SAUCE

3 oz. sugar

3 oz. water

$1/4$ cup cream

2 oz. whole butter

Combine sugar and water in small saucepan and whisk until dissolved. Bring to a boil. When sugar is golden brown, remove from heat and let cool 5 minutes. Add cream and butter. Whisk continually until well incorporated. Set aside and keep warm.

CARAMELIZED BANANAS

- 2 oz. whole butter
- 4 bananas (sliced)
- 2 Tbs. dried currants
- 1 oz. sugar
- 2 Tbs. chocolate chips
- 1/2 tsp. ground cinnamon for garnish

Melt whole butter in a nonstick pan over medium heat; combine bananas and currants with 1 ounce sugar and cook until golden brown (approximately 2 minutes). At the last moment, add chocolate chips. Remove from stove. Set aside, keeping warm.

To Serve

Sprinkle ground cinnamon around the border of a large serving plate. Place 2 tablespoons of banana mixture in center of plate. Place phyllo layer on top. Place another 2 tablespoons of bananas on top of phyllo and finish with one more layer of phyllo. Pour 3 tablespoons of caramel sauce around Millefeuille. Serve immediately.

STYLE

(Not) Another Boring Day in Paradise

white plates, creating contrast and charm. Match napkins to the color of the place mats and plates, and finish the setting with clear stemware for water and wine. Of course, the food is part of the presentation.

The elements of this beautiful table are the essence of simplicity and function: Start with a grape leaf centerpiece with fruit and add a gossamer runner to give the table texture and style.

Napa plates with an intricate pattern serve as nests for simple

Add a bottle of your favorite wine, some fruit and cheese served on green marble, and you are ready for your guests.

KEVIN CULLEN

GOODFELLOW'S
MINNEAPOLIS, MINNESOTA

APPETIZERS

SOCKEYE SALMON MARTINI
WITH NECTARINE-PEANUT SALSA

CHILLED BEET, CARROT, AND
BUNYATO SOUP WITH PLANTAIN
CHIPS AND MANGO RELISH

ENTRÉES

GARLIC ROAST PHEASANT OR
CHICKEN WITH BLUE CHEESE
POLENTA AND CÈPE MUSH-
ROOMS

GRILLED LAMB CHOPS WITH
POTATO SALAD LASAGNA AND
BARBECUE SWEET CORN

DESSERT

CHILLED SUMMER FRUIT SOUP
WITH SESAME ICE CREAM

"The best aspect of being a chef is creating totally original dishes: spicy and mild, sweet and sour. It's a total experience of yin and yang, yet these dishes are soothing to the palate," says Executive Chef Kevin Cullen of Goodfellow's in downtown Minneapolis. Goodfellow's serves "seasonal-regional American cuisine," the choicest local and regional products accentuated with spice from the deep South and Far East.

Chef Cullen was raised in the Minneapolis suburbs of Coon Rapids and New Brighton. He received his culinary training in Anoka, another Minneapolis suburb. Prior to being named Sous Chef at La Torte restaurant in 1981, Chef Cullen worked in the kitchens of McGuire's Inn in St. Paul and the Anchorage Restaurant at the Hilton Hotel in Minneapolis. Two years later he moved to Texas, where he served as Executive Sous Chef at the Carlisle Restaurant in Houston and then as Executive Chef at the Victoria Plaza Club in Victoria. In 1986, Chef Cullen accepted the Sous Chef position at the highly acclaimed Mansion on Turtle Creek Restaurant in Dallas. A year later, Cullen was invited to return to his home state and serve as Executive Sous Chef for the newly opened Goodfellow's Restaurant. In 1992, Chef Cullen was named Executive Chef at Goodfellow's.

In 1993, Cullen received a Taste of Elegance Award from the Minnesota Pork Producers and a Superior Chef Award from the National Pork Producers. Later that year, Chef Cullen's entry was one of six chosen out of 100 as an Evian Water/*Gourmet* magazine Healthy Heart Award winner for the Midwest Division. Chef Cullen has also been one of ten top chefs who completely revamped Northwest Airlines' in-flight menus.

Kevin lives in Circle Pines, Minnesota with his wife Patti and their three children, Candice, Neil, and Matt.

PHOTO: *Garlic roast pheasant with blue cheese polenta and cèpe mushrooms*

SOCKEYE SALMON MARTINI WITH NECTARINE-PEANUT SALSA

(Serves 6)

NECTARINE-PEANUT SALSA

1   cup nectarines, diced

3   oz. fresh orange juice

2   oz. peanuts or cashews, chopped

1   Tbs. chopped shiso or cilantro

2   red jalapenos, minced

1   clove garlic, minced

1   lime, juiced

1   tsp. ginger juice

3   Tbs. peanut oil

Splash of fish sauce

Salt to taste

Combine salsa ingredients and allow to let stand.

SALMON

Cut the salmon into $1^1/_2$-ounce pieces and skewer with either wooden skewers or herb stalks. Rub the salmon pieces with peanut oil to keep the meat from sticking to the grill. Place skewered salmon on the grill, and cook to medium rare, turning once. Remove from heat and let stand for several minutes.

To Serve

Place 6 ounces of nectarine-peanut salsa in a martini glass and top with a salmon skewer. Serve immediately.

CHILLED BEET, CARROT, AND BUNYATO SOUPS WITH PLANTAIN CHIPS AND MANGO RELISH

(Serves 20)

ROASTED BEET SOUP

$1^3/_4$ cups beets, roasted, peeled, and sliced
$^1/_2$ cup red onion, sliced
$^1/_2$ cup raspberry vinegar
2   red jalapeños
1   qt. chicken stock

Roast beets in a 375°F oven until skin shrinks and the beets are soft inside. Remove from heat, peel, and slice. Place beets in a saucepan and add the onion, jalepeños, vinegar, and chicken stock. Simmer over medium heat until cooked through. Remove from heat and purée until mixture is smooth. Pour mixture through a china cap (cone-shaped strainer). Using a wooden spoon, press mixture through the strainer to ensure all liquid has been strained. Place in refrigerator to chill.

CARROT-GINGER SOUP

$1^3/_4$ cups sweet carrots, peeled and sliced
$^1/_2$ yellow bell pepper
$^1/_2$ cup jewel yams, peeled and sliced
$^1/_2$ cup yellow onion, sliced
$^1/_2$ cup ginger, peeled and sliced
1   qt. chicken stock
1   clove garlic

Peel and slice carrots. Cut the bell pepper in half and remove the core. Place the carrots, bell pepper half, sliced yams, onion, ginger, and garlic in the chicken stock and simmer over medium heat until cooked through. Remove from heat and purée until mixture is smooth. Pour mixture through a china cap. Using a wooden spoon press mixture through the strainer to ensure all liquid has been strained. Place in refrigerator to chill.

BUNYATO SOUP

$1^3/_4$ cups bunyatos, peeled and sliced
1   cup sliced leek (white portion only)
2   cloves garlic, sliced
2   serrano chilies, sliced
1   qt. chicken stock
1   cup butter

Place all ingredients in a saucepan with the chicken stock and simmer until cooked through. Remove from heat and purée in a blender until mixture is smooth. Pour mixture through a china cap. Using a wooden spoon press mixture through the strainer to ensure all liquid has been strained. Set aside.

MANGO RELISH

2   cups mango, diced
1   cup jicama, diced
$^1/_4$ cup chives, sliced
2   oranges, juiced
2   limes, juiced
Salt to taste

Place mango, jicama, and chives in a bowl. Squeeze juices over mango mixture and season to taste. Place in refrigerator until ready for service.

GARNISH

40   plantain chips

Peel and thinly slice green plantains lengthwise. Fry in hot oil until crispy. Remove from oil, place on paper towels to absorb the excess oil, and salt lightly. Set aside to cool.

To Serve

This step will require two people. In a chilled soup bowl, ladle 2 ounces each of the beet, carrot ginger, and bunyato soups simultaneously. The finished result will have each of the soups covering $1/3$ of the bowl. Garnish with the mango relish and plantain chips and serve.

GARLIC ROAST PHEASANT WITH BLUE CHEESE POLENTA AND CÈPE MUSHROOMS

(Serves 6)

BLUE CHEESE POLENTA

1	cup cornmeal (finely ground)
3	cups chicken stock
2	tsp. minced garlic
$1/2$	cup mixed herbs
$1/2$	cup romano cheese
$3/4$	cup blue cheese, crumbled

Salt and pepper to taste

Place cornmeal, garlic, and stock in double boiler and cook on high for 30 to 40 minutes. Fold in herbs and romano cheese. Remove from heat and season to taste. Spoon into a greased baking dish and place in refrigerator uncovered until chilled.

GARLIC ROAST PHEASANT (OR CHICKEN)

6	pheasant (or chicken) breasts, skin on
$3/4$	cup chopped garlic in olive oil
	Peanut oil
	Salt and pepper

Season breasts with salt and pepper. Brush garlic on breasts. In a hot pan with peanut oil, sear breasts on both sides. Remove from pan and place in 375°F oven. Roast until cooked (30 to 50 minutes). Remove from oven and let stand for a few minutes.

PHOTO: *Sockeye salmon martini with a nectarine-peanut salsa*

CÈPE JUICE

1	lb. cèpe mushrooms
3	Tbs. olive oil
1	cup red wine
$1/2$	cup shallot, sliced

Clean cèpe mushrooms. Sauté in olive oil. Add shallots and glaze with red wine. Reduce by half. Remove from heat and set aside for service.

To Serve

Cut polenta into desired shape and place blue cheese on top. Bake at 350°F until cheese melts. Place polenta on plate. Slice breast and fan over polenta. Pour cèpe mushrooms with juice over chicken. Serve immediately.

Wine Recommendation:
Matanzas Creek Chardonnay

ΜΑΤΑΝΖΑS CREEK WINERY

GRILLED LAMB CHOPS WITH POTATO SALAD LASAGNA AND BARBECUE SWEET CORN

(Serves 6)

LAMB CHOPS

12	lamb chops

Cut lamb into chops or have a butcher do this step.

DRESSING

1	cup mayonnaise
$1/2$	cup buttermilk
1	clove garlic, minced
1	tsp. red chili flakes

1   tsp. fresh ground fennel (or anise seed)

$^1/_2$ lime, juiced

1   tsp. cracked black pepper

Place all ingredients in a blender and pulse until well mixed. Transfer mixture to a clean bowl and set aside.

POTATO SALAD LASAGNA BASE

$^1/_3$ cup ham, chopped

$^1/_2$ cup eggs, chopped

$^1/_3$ cup celery, minced

$^1/_3$ cup red onion, minced

$^1/_2$ cup fennel, sliced

$^1/_2$ cup mustard greens, sliced

$^1/_3$ cup blue cheese, crumbled

Place all ingredients in a large bowl. Add dressing and fold together, making sure all ingredients are well coated. Season to taste and set aside.

POTATO SALAD LASAGNA

2   potatoes

2   yams

3   Tbs. olive oil

Square off potatoes and yams and slice 12 each, $^1/_4$-inch-thick slices. Brush with olive oil on both sides and roast in a 350°F oven until tender. Remove from heat and let cool. Once cooled to room temperature, lay a piece of potato square on a plate. Spoon a layer of the base on the potato and lay a yam square on top. Spoon on another layer of base and place in refrigerator until ready for service.

BARBECUE CORN RELISH

16 ears roasted corn, cut off the cob

$^1/_2$ cup tomatillo, diced

$^1/_2$ cup red onion, diced

1   cup barbecue sauce

1   Tbs. marjoram, chopped

2   green jalapeño peppers, minced

Worcester, salt, and Tabasco to taste

Roast corn in the husk. Remove corn from heat, remove husks, and clean corn. Cut kernels off the cob. Mix corn with the rest of the ingredients and season to taste. (Note: thin out barbecue sauce with water if it is too thick.)

To Serve

Grill lamb to desired temperature and remove from heat. Let stand 3 minutes. Place potato salad lasagna square and lamb chops on a plate. Spoon barbecue corn relish over chops and garnish with fresh herbs. Serve immediately.

CHILLED SUMMER FRUIT SOUP WITH SESAME ICE CREAM

(Serves 6)

SUMMER FRUIT

4   plums (black beauty or Queen Ann)

$^1/_2$ lb. cherries

1   pt. strawberries

1   pt. blackberries

Slice fruit and place in a bowl. Set aside.

SYRUP

$2^1/_2$ cups water

1   cup sugar

2   oranges, juiced (or 1 cup plum wine)

4   pieces star anise

1   cinnamon stick

Small piece of ginger root

Place all ingredients in a small saucepan and bring to a boil. Make sure all sugar is dissolved. Remove from heat and chill over ice or in refrigerator. When syrup is very cool, pour over summer fruit and fold gently. Cover and return to refrigerator for 10 hours or overnight.

SESAME BRITTLE

2   cups sugar
1   cup water
$^1/_4$ tsp. cream of tartar
$1^1/_2$ cup roasted sesame seeds

Place sugar, water, and cream of tartar in a heavy saucepan over high heat and stir until mixed. Boil to a hard crack and remove from heat. Fold in the sesame seeds and pour onto a greased cookie sheet. Let cool and break into small pieces. Add desired amount to ice cream. Store unused portion in a cool dry place.

SESAME ICE CREAM

(Yields 2 quarts)

12   egg yolks
3   cups milk
$^1/_2$ vanilla bean
$1^1/_2$ cup sugar
4   Tbs. roasted sesame seeds
2   cups heavy whipping cream

Whip yolks until they are light yellow and frothy. Heat milk and sugar in a heavy saucepan, stirring gently. Split and scrape vanilla bean in milk and sugar combination. Add roasted sesame seeds and scald. Add 1 cup hot mixture to the yolks (be careful not to add too fast or the yolks will scramble). Whisk together and place in double boiler. Cook slowly until mixture coats a spoon, then place over ice and chill. Add heavy whipping cream. After mixture is cool, place in ice cream machine and freeze according to instructions. When frozen, fold in sesame brittle.

To Serve

Chill 6 martini glasses. Ladle summer fruit soup into the martini glasses and float a scoop of the sesame ice cream on top.

WINE

Wines of the World

Americans tend to drink a lot of Chardonnay, Cabernet Sauvignon, Merlot, and Sauvignon Blanc. But we should also experiment with wines from around the world. There are great wines from Germany's Rhone district, where they are creating great Sirahs and Rieslings, and some fabulous Australian and Chilean wines available that have slightly different styles than California varietals. Many believe California wines are as good as, if not better than, those grown in France. California probably has more vintage years because of its consistent, temperate, and relatively drier climate.

STYLE

Wonders of the World

For reminiscences of travels past or anticipation of travels planned, create a special evening for friends. Use hunter green napkins that match your place mats as the nest for a centerpiece—in this case plants and flowers selected to be both familiar and exotic. Add tall candles for elegance and warmth, and create a fun pocket for the silverware by folding a contrasting or complementary napkin and slipping the silverware inside. Small globes or travel guides stir the wanderlust, and plates with colored rims create elegant place settings. Complete the table by adding green-tinted stemware.

SANFORD D'AMATO

SANFORD
MILWAUKEE, WISCONSIN

APPETIZERS

SKATE SALAD WITH LOCAL
TOMATOES, SORREL, AND
CAPER VINAIGRETTE

CHAR-GRILLED ASPARAGUS
AND WILD MUSHROOMS WITH
ITALIAN PARSLEY ESSENCE ON
CORN, LEEK, AND POTATO
CAKE

ENTRÉES

CORIANDER-CRUSTED STRIP-
LOIN OF BEEF ON LENTIL
AND BASMATI SALAD WITH
CORIANDER OIL

SALMON ON SEARED RAPINI
WITH SAFFRON LIMA BEAN
BROTH

DESSERT

GINGER-SNAP CANNOLI WITH
WISCONSIN DRIED CHERRY
AND MASCARPONE CREAM

"A kitchen is an orchestra and the chef a conductor. A good conductor has a knowledge of all the instruments and should play them as well as the musicians. That knowledge helps to coordinate the instruments so everything comes out right," says Executive Chef/Owner Sandy D'Amato of Sanford Restaurant in Milwaukee, Wisconsin.

Chef D'Amato, a Milwaukee native, graduated from the Culinary Institute of America in New York in 1974. He continued for a one-year fellowship in the Escoffier Room under the direction of Peter Van Erp. Throughout the seventies, D'Amato worked in various restaurants in New York City and Long Island. It was there that he began thinking of his Milwaukee roots and a gentler pace.

In 1980, Chef D'Amato returned to Milwaukee and worked in the kitchen of John Byron's, where he met his wife and partner, Angie. After Sandy's nine years as Executive Chef, Sandy and Angie decided to set out on their own. They bought the D'Amato family grocery building, the site of his grandfather's and father's grocery store where Sandy lived the first three years of his life.

In 1985, D'Amato received national attention when *Food & Wine* magazine included him on their list of the top 25 "Hot New Chefs." In 1988, he was hailed as "one of the finest seafood chefs in the country" in a *Bon Appetit* feature article. Chef D'Amato received one of two gold medals and took third overall in the 1988 and 1989 American Seafood Challenge. In 1992, Chef D'Amato was personally chosen by Julia Child to be one of twelve chefs in the nation to cook for her eightieth birthday celebration in Boston. On April 29, 1996, Chef D'Amato was awarded the coveted Pierre Jouet's Best Chef Midwest by the James Beard Foundation in New York.

PHOTO: *Coriander-crusted striploin of beef on lentil and basmati salad with coriander oil*

SKATE SALAD WITH LOCAL TOMATOES, SORREL, AND CAPER VINAIGRETTE

(Serves 4)

CAPER VINAIGRETTE

1	head garlic (approximately 3 oz.) tossed in 1 Tbs. olive oil and roasted in a 400°F oven for 30 minutes
1/4	cup extra virgin olive oil
3/4	cup regular olive oil
2	Tbs. small capers
2	tsp. kosher salt
1/2	tsp. freshly ground black pepper
1/4	tsp. cayenne pepper
1	Tbs. lemon juice
2	tsp. balsamic vinegar

When garlic is cool, break up the head and squeeze the garlic cloves out of the skins into a small blender. Add all ingredients except the capers and blend until garlic is totally puréed. Add capers and transfer to a squeeze bottle with a tip large enough to let the capers pass through. This portion of the dish can be made ahead of time.

SKATE SALAD

1 1/2	lbs. skate wing, skinned or 1 lb. boneless and skinless skate
1/4	cup olive oil
2	local yellow tomatoes, med. to lg. size
2	local red tomatoes, med. to lg. size
24	leaves of fresh sorrel
1	bunch of watercress

Kosher salt and fresh ground black pepper
Caper vinaigrette
Flour to dust skate

Divide the skate into 4 portions. Trim tomatoes and cut into 6 nice slices each, for a total of 24 slices, and reserve. Get a large nonstick sauté pan (large enough to hold the skate without crowding) very hot. Season skate with salt and pepper, flour lightly, and shake off excess. Add oil to pan and sauté skate quickly until golden brown (about 2 minutes per side).

To Serve

Intersperse 3 slices of red and 3 slices of yellow tomatoes in a circle on a plate. Place 1 piece of sorrel between each slice. Season with salt and pepper and dress each plate with approximately 2 tablespoons of the shaken caper dressing. Place skate in the center of tomatoes and garnish with the seasoned watercress and caper vinaigrette.

CHAR-GRILLED ASPARAGUS AND WILD MUSHROOMS WITH ITALIAN PARSLEY ESSENCE ON CORN, LEEK, AND POTATO CAKE

(Serves 4)

CHAR-GRILLED ASPARAGUS

1	lb. med. asparagus, trimmed, peeled
1	lb. lg. chanterelles, stems trimmed and reserved (other wild mushrooms may be substituted)
1/2	cup extra virgin olive oil
1/3	cup lemon juice

Blanch asparagus in boiling salted water for 15 seconds. Remove from heat and immediately shock in ice water. Drain and reserve. Marinate mushrooms in olive oil and lemon juice for 15 minutes; asparagus will be added to this mixture just prior to grilling.

ITALIAN PARSLEY AND MUSHROOM ESSENCE

1	Tbs. olive oil
1	Tbs. chopped shallots and reserved cleaned mushroom stems, chopped fine
1 1/2	cups dry vermouth
1	bunch Italian parsley, leaves only
3/4	cup olive oil
1/2	tsp. salt
1/4	tsp. freshly ground pepper

Sauté shallots and mushroom stems in olive oil for about 2 minutes. Add dry vermouth and reduce to about $1/4$ cup of strained liquid. Add liquid to a blender with the remaining ingredients and blend until smooth. Place in plastic squeeze bottle and refrigerate until needed.

CORN LEEK AND POTATO CAKE

2   lbs. Idaho potatoes
2   ears of corn, shucked, oiled with 1 Tbs. olive oil, grilled for 8 minutes, then cut off the cob
5   oz. (1 lg.) trimmed leek, cleaned and sliced thin
1   tsp. chopped garlic
$1/2$ Tbs. chopped shallot
$1/4$ tsp. fresh ground pepper
$1/2$ Tbs. kosher salt
Pinch of nutmeg
$1/2$ cup heavy cream
4   Tbs. olive oil

Bake potatoes in 400°F oven for approximately 1 hour until tender. Meanwhile, sauté leeks in 2 tablespoons olive oil for about 1 to 2 minutes. Add shallots, sauté 30 seconds, and add garlic and corn kernels. (If you don't grill corn on cob, sauté corn kernels first for 2 minutes before adding leeks.) Add nutmeg and heavy cream. Bring to a boil, remove from heat, and transfer to a stainless bowl. When potatoes are done, scoop the potato flesh into a food mill or ricer and pass the flesh into the corn and leek bowl. Fold together all ingredients. Heat a 10-inch nonstick sauté pan; place $1/2$ of remaining olive oil in pan and place potato cake in pan. Even out and sauté over low to medium heat for about 10 minutes. Place a cookie sheet over the sauté pan and carefully invert cake onto the cookie sheet. Add remaining oil to the pan and slide cake back into sauté pan. Sauté 8 to 10 more minutes until golden on both sides. Once again invert on cookie sheet and reserve in a warm place.

PICKLED GRILLED RED ONIONS

1   lg. red onion, peeled and sliced thin
$1/4$ cup olive oil
$1/2$ cup red wine vinegar
$3/4$ cup water
$1^1/2$ Tbs. sugar
1   tsp. kosher salt
5   peppercorns
1   sprig rosemary
2   garlic cloves
3   whole allspice
1   cinnamon stick
2   bay leaves
1   sprig thyme

On a hot grill, brush onion slices with oil and grill for 30 to 60 seconds on each side until crisp and tender. Place into a bowl. Bring vinegar, water, sugar, and salt to a boil. Add remaining ingredients wrapped in a sachet or cheesecloth. Let steep, covered, for 30 minutes. Pour over onions and marinate at least 1 hour (preferably overnight).

To Serve

Add asparagus to mushrooms in marinade. Season with kosher salt and freshly ground pepper. Place on hot grill and grill 1 to 2 minutes per side until well colored but not overcooked. Cut potato cake into 8 pieces. Place 2 pieces on each plate. Arrange asparagus and mushrooms on potato cake. Garnish with parsley-mushroom essence and pickled red onions.

CORIANDER-CRUSTED STRIPLOIN OF BEEF ON LENTIL AND BASMATI SALAD WITH CORIANDER OIL

(Serves 4)

BEEF MARINADE

4   8-oz. center-cut prime striploins, trimmed of all fat
$1^1/2$ oz. shallots, peeled and sliced thin
$1/2$ oz. garlic, peeled and sliced thin
1   oz. lemon juice
$1/2$ cup white wine
$1/2$ bunch cilantro, chopped in $1/2$-inch pieces, stems and all
$1/4$ cup corn oil

In a large bowl, add all ingredients together. Add striploins, making sure each is well coated. Reserve.

BASMATI RICE
2   oz. onions, diced brunoise
1   cup basmati rice
1¹/₂ cups chicken stock, brought up to a boil with salt and pepper
1   bay leaf
¹/₂ Tbs. black cumin seeds
¹/₄ cup olive oil
Salt and pepper to taste

Sauté onions in hot oil until translucent. Add bay leaf and cumin seeds. Sauté for 3 minutes and add rice, stirring to ensure all kernels are coated. Sauté. Add stock and bring up to a boil. Cut parchment paper to the size of the saucepan and coat with oil. Cover rice with the oiled paper and bake 15 to 20 minutes at 350 to 375°F.

LENTILS
3/4 cup small Indian brown lentils (with water to cover by 2 inches)
4   cloves garlic
¹/₂ carrot
¹/₂ stalk celery
1   sm. whole onion, peeled
¹/₂ Tbs. black cumin seeds, toasted
1   sprig thyme
Kosher salt and freshly ground black pepper to taste

In a dry pan over medium heat, toast cumin seeds until they become fragrant and begin to pop. Add carrot, celery, onion, and all spices to the lentils and cook half-covered until tender. Drain and reserve.

BLACK CUMIN MUSTARD DRESSING
1   egg yolk, room temperature
1¹/₄ oz. hot mustard, dissolved in 1/4 cup hot water

1   cup olive oil
3   Tbs. vinegar
1¹/₂ tsp. ground roasted black cumin seeds
Salt and freshly ground black pepper to taste
Water to thin

Place egg yolk, mustard, and ¹/₂ of the vinegar in mini food processor. Add oil slowly. Add vinegar and seasoning. Adjust thickness with water.

CILANTRO OIL
1   bunch cilantro
2   cloves garlic, peeled and diced
³/₄ cup olive oil
¹/₄ tsp. salt
10 grinds freshly ground black pepper

Pick leaves from cilantro (reserve about ¹/₄ the bunch for garnish). Add remaining leaves to a blender with remaining ingredients and purée completely. Place in a plastic squeeze bottle and reserve.

LEMON AND OLIVE OIL DRESSING
1   cup olive oil
1   lemon, juiced
Salt and freshly ground black pepper to taste

SPICE MIX
2   Tbs. whole fennel seeds
2   Tbs. coriander seeds
1   tsp. kosher salt
¹/₂ tsp. white peppercorns

Toast seeds and pepper until fragrant. Grind coarse in spice mill with salt. Use to season meat just before cooking. Coat striploins with spice mixture and cook in a medium-hot pan in 2 tablespoons of olive oil for 3 to 4 minutes. Turn and cook to desired doneness. Let rest for 3 minutes.

GARNISH
1   seedless cucumber
Lemon dressing
Salt and pepper

Trim seedless cucumbers with a channel knife for decoration and thinly slice. Season cucumber slices with lemon dressing and salt and pepper.

To Serve

Mix lentils and rice with cilantro oil and lemon dressing. Place on a plate with cucumbers. Cut meat on the bias and fan beef over lentil and rice. Garnish with cilantro oil, mustard dressing, and cilantro leaves.

Wine recommendation:
Murietta's Well Vendemia Red

SALMON ON SEARED RAPINI WITH SAFFRON LIMA BEAN BROTH

(Serves 4)

SAFFRON LIMA BEANS

1	cup or 6 oz. dry lima beans (rinse, place in a container and cover with 4 cups of very hot water; cover and refrigerate overnight)
$^1/_4$	onion
$^1/_2$	sm. leek
$^1/_2$	celery stalk
2	Tbs. kosher salt
$^1/_2$	tsp. saffron threads
1	qt. cold water
$1^1/_2$	cups unsalted chicken stock

Place the following in a cheesecloth sachet:

6	lg. cloves garlic
2	whole cloves
3	whole star anise
40	peppercorns, crushed
2	sprigs fresh thyme
2	bay leaves

Drain beans and place in a 3-quart. sauce pot. Tie the onion, leek, and celery stalk together with string. Add vegetables and sachet of spices. Add water, saffron, and salt. Bring up to a boil and cook at a semi-rapid simmer $^3/_4$ covered for about 35 to 45 minutes, until beans are tender and creamy inside but not falling apart. Drain beans. Cool and reserve liquid. Mix $1^1/_2$ cups of bean broth with $1^1/_2$ cups of chicken stock. Check for seasoning and reserve.

RAPINI

1	bunch rapini (about 12 oz.)
2	Tbs. olive oil
$^1/_2$	tsp. garlic, chopped
1	tsp. shallot, chopped
	Salt and pepper to taste

Peel tough rapini stems. Chop stems about $^1/_8$-inch thick. Keep separate from tops. Chop tops $^1/_2$-inch thick. Heat a 12-inch sauté pan very hot. Add oil and rapini stems, sauté 20 seconds. Add garlic and shallots, sauté 10 seconds. Add tops and sauté for 45 seconds to 1 minute until crisp and tender. Add salt and pepper to taste. Immediately cool in refrigerator until needed.

GLAZED GARLIC AND ORANGE GARNISH

	Long zest of 1 large orange
8–10	lg. cloves garlic, sliced and julienned
1	cup water
1	tsp. sugar
1	tsp. olive oil
1	tsp. Italian parsley, chopped
	Pinch of salt

Place garlic and orange zest in pan of water. Bring to a boil for 5 seconds and strain. Refresh in cold water. Strain well. Bring a nonstick sauté pan to high heat. Add olive oil and garlic and orange mixture. Add salt and sugar and sauté for 30 to 45 seconds over high heat. Add 1 teaspoon chopped Italian parsley and remove to a plate and cool. Reserve.

SALMON

4	6 to 7 oz. skinless salmon fillets (preferably 4" x 4"x 1" thick)
1/4	cup regular olive oil
	Flour to dust
	Salt and freshly ground black pepper

Season fillets with salt and pepper. Lightly dredge in flour. Pat off excess flour. Sauté in a 12-inch hot sauté pan in olive oil, 3 to 4 minutes per side for 1-inch thick filets, until golden.

To Serve

Heat up beans and broth. Add 2 tablespoons chiffonade of Italian parsley to beans. Divide warm rapini between 4 large soup bowls. Place cooked salmon filet on top of rapini, surround with beans, and pour broth over salmon. Garnish with glazed garlic and orange zest.

GINGER-SNAP CANNOLI WITH WISCONSIN DRIED CHERRY AND MASCARPONE CREAM

(Serves 4)

GINGER-SNAP CANNOLI SHELLS

1	oz. sugar
1	oz. butter
1/2	tsp. ground ginger
1	oz. dark corn syrup
1/4	tsp. lemon juice
1	oz. flour
1	20" x 1 1/4" thick wooden dowel or similar size rolling pin

Combine all ingredients except flour in a small stainless steel bowl. Place bowl in a double boiler. Melt everything slowly at a low simmer. Mix periodically with a whisk. When blended and warm, add flour and stir in with a spatula. Preheat oven to 375°F. Put the warm mixture into a pastry bag with a #2 round tip (before filling, push part of the pastry bag into the tip to prevent mixture from running out when filling). Pipe mixture onto a parchment paper-lined cookie sheet (put a dab of mixture under each corner to hold down paper). Pipe mixture in a 4-inch circle in a spiral motion toward center. Hold tip 1/4-inch off paper to control thickness and leave 1/4-inch open space between spiral; spaces will fill in while baking. Ginger snaps should be fairly thin when finished. Bake for 2

minutes, turn the cookie sheet around, and bake 3 more minutes or until golden brown. Take out of the oven and not immediately, but while they are still warm (about 45 to 60 seconds) form them around the dowel in a tube shape (dowel should be suspended from work surface in some fashion and should be ready prior to baking). If they are too hard to form, place them back in the oven for 30 seconds and repeat process. Carefully remove cannoli shells from the dowel. They will be fragile. Shells can be made ahead and stored in a covered container in a cool, dry place.

FILLING

(Ingredients must be cold before mixing)

4	oz. Wisconsin mascarpone cheese
1/2	orange, finely zested
1	oz. bourbon
1	Tbs. sugar
2	Tbs. dried currants
2	Tbs. Door County dried cherries, coarsely chopped
1/4	cup softened pastry cream (recipe below)
1/4	cup heavy cream, whipped to soft peaks
1 1/2	tsp. Grand Marnier
3	Tbs. roasted, chopped pistachios
	Confectioners' sugar

Reduce bourbon, zest, sugar, currants, and cherries in a nonstick pan, stirring until almost dry. Cool in refrigerator. When cold, add mixture to mascarpone with a rubber spatula. Mix together. Add the pastry cream and mix. Add Grand Marnier and mix. Fold in the whipped cream; be careful not to overmix. Place in a pastry bag with a #18 tip and fill the cannoli shells. Dip the ends of filled shells in the pistachios and dust exterior with confectioners' sugar.

PASTRY CREAM

1/2	cup milk
1	oz. sugar
1	egg yolk
1/4	oz. cornstarch
	Dash of vanilla

Bring milk and 1/2 of the sugar to a boil in a small noncorro-

PHOTO: *Ginger-snap cannoli with Wisconsin dried cherry and mascarpone cream*

sive pot. In a separate bowl, whip egg yolk with the rest of the sugar until light colored. Whip in cornstarch and vanilla. Slowly whip in the hot milk and sugar mixture. Return mixture to the pot and continue whipping while bringing it to a boil so that mixture does not stick to the bottom. Let boil for 30 seconds and place in a clean bowl. Cover loosely with plastic wrap and refrigerate.

VERBENA ICE CREAM

2 oz. verbena, leaves only (substitute mint)

Place in half and half mixture from the ice cream recipe below and simmer for $1/2$ hour. Strain into yolks and proceed with recipe.

ICE CREAM BASE
7   egg yolks
$^1/_2$ cup sugar
$1^3/_4$ cups heavy cream
$^3/_4$ cups half and half

WINE

Chardonnay in America

Ernest A. Wente was instrumental in developing Chardonnay vineyards in California. Chardonnay has now become one of the backbone varietals of the state. In the early 1900s, Professor Bonet at the University of California at Davis whose brother ran a world-famous nursery in France, suggested that the Wentes grow Chardonnay. They arranged for cuttings to be sent from France, planted them in the Livermore Valley, and began to propagate them. Today, nearly eighty percent of all the vines planted to Chardonnay are from the "Wente Clone."

Serving a crisp, dry white wine such as a Chardonnay with fish acts very much like a wedge of lemon as the acid of the wine cuts through the "fishiness" and enhances the flavor.

Whisk the egg yolks and half of the sugar in a bowl to blend. Bring remaining sugar and half and half to a boil in a saucepan. Gradually whisk the half and half mixture into the egg yolks. Return mixture to saucepan and stir over medium heat until custard thickens and leaves path on back of spoon when finger is drawn across. Strain custard into a bowl that is sitting in an ice bath. Add heavy cream and, when cool, add various flavorings and freeze in an ice cream machine.

DESSERT SAUCE
1   mango or papaya, chopped
$2^1/_2$ limes, juiced
In a food processor, add the chopped mango or papaya and lime juice and liquefy.

LEMON POPPY SEED WAFERS
$1^1/_2$ Tbs. sugar
$1^1/_2$ Tbs. poppy seeds
$^1/_2$ lemon
1   Tbs. butter
1   Tbs. plus 1 tsp. egg white
$1^1/_2$ Tbs. flour

Combine all ingredients except flour in a bowl. Fold in the flour; do not overmix. Allow batter to rest for 1 hour. On a baking sheet lined with parchment paper, spread 1 teaspoon batter with a small spatula in a circle about 3 inches around per wafer. Bake in a 350 to 375°F oven until golden brown. When still warm, place each wafer over a rolling pin or in a tuille pan to shape. When cool, reserve in a covered container in one layer.

To Serve
Place the cannoli on mango-lime sauce and accompany with verbena ice cream in a poppy seed wafer.

STYLE

Another Year Younger

For that birthday celebration, we start with a simple wooden table covered in a white cloth upon which are placed wildflowers in velvet and colorful die-cut bags. Add decorative or real presents to set the theme. Multicolored place mats add whimsy. Select plates with a pattern that complements the place mats and has special meaning to the birthday guest.

Cobalt blue glasses match blue napkins. Birthday parties require curling ribbons with lots of ruffles and flourishes. On the sideboard: more presents, preparations for dessert, and, of course, we continue the color and floral themes from the table.

ELLEN GREAVES

THE TEA BOX CAFE AT TAKASHIMAYA
NEW YORK, NEW YORK

APPETIZER
CURRIED CRAB ROLL WITH
ARUGULA AND CHINESE BLACK
BEAN VINAIGRETTE

ENTRÉES
GLAZED CHICKEN BREAST WITH
MESCLUN AND DAIKON RADISH

SPICE-CRUSTED PORK TENDER-
LOIN WITH DAIKON RADISH

SAKE-POACHED COD WITH
QUINOA AND SHIITAKES

DESSERT
WARM WINTER FRUIT COMPOTE
OF QUINCE, PRUNES, AND
APRICOTS SOAKED IN EARL
GREY TEA AND ORANGES

"A unique experience in cross-cultural cuisine" is the description on the front of the menu for the Tea Box Cafe at Takashimaya, the elegant department store located in the heart of Fifth Avenue's shopping district in New York City. Canadian-born Executive Chef Ellen Greaves's artistic and unexpected combinations of East and West are considered essential to the spirit of the cafe.

An honor graduate from La Varenne École de Cuisine of Paris and the Stratford Chef's School in Canada, Chef Greaves's experience is diverse: she has worked in the kitchens at Rundles, Stadtlander's, The Quilted Giraffe, Langan's Brasserie, La Colombe D'Or, March Restaurant, and Winston's. Chef Greaves teamed with Gary Goldberg, director of the Culinary Center of New York, and Elizabeth Andoh, consultant and Japanese cookbook author, to develop the Cafe's luncheon and tea menus, which feature original American cuisine with a Japanese flair. While the Tea Box is only open for lunch and afternoon tea, Chef Greaves's menu is intriguing and masterful. The centerpiece dish, the Tea Box Bento, is a square box with four compartments of seasonal treats of seafood, meats or poultry, salads, and a flavored rice.

Chef Ellen Greaves has coauthored with Wayne Nish, chef/owner of March Restaurant, a soon-to-be-released book on her Bento boxes.

PHOTO: *Curried crab roll with arugula and Chinese black bean vinaigrette*

CURRIED CRAB ROLL WITH ARUGULA AND CHINESE BLACK BEAN VINAIGRETTE
(Serves 4)

CURRIED CRAB ROLLS

$1/2$ lb. fresh crab meat

$1/4$ cup mayonnaise

$1/2$ Tbs. ground turmeric

1   tsp. cumin

$3/8$ tsp. cayenne pepper

$1/2$ tsp. salt

1   fresh red pepper, cut into julienne strips

2   cups snow pea shoots (if unavailable you may use spinach leaves)

1   pack 8-inch diameter Vietnamese spring roll wrappers (also known as Thai rice paper wrappers)

Fresh ground pepper

Warm water

Mix the crab with the mayonnaise, turmeric, cumin, cayenne pepper, salt, and pepper. Soak a spring roll paper wrapper in warm water until soft (approximately 2 minutes). (If the water is too cold the wrapper will take too long to get soft, and if it is too warm the wrappers will get soft too quickly.) Work on a damp towel. Place a soft spring roll wrapper (it should feel like a well-worn dollar bill) on the towel. On the third closest to you place a line of snow pea shoots. Place $1/5$ of the crab mixture on top of the snow pea shoots and then a line of red pepper strips. Roll the wrapper up tightly and keep covered in the refrigerator. Repeat with the rest of the crab, making 5 rolls in all. (If wrapped individually in plastic, the crab rolls can be made up to 12 hours in advance.)

CHINESE BLACK BEAN VINAIGRETTE

1   tsp. sugar

$1/2$ tsp. salt

2   Tbs. brown rice vinegar

$1^1/2$ Tbs. sake

6   Tbs. extra virgin olive oil

$1^1/2$ Tbs. Chinese preserved black beans (also called fermented black beans)

1   bunch arugula, washed and trimmed to bite-sized pieces

Whisk together the sugar, salt, vinegar, and sake. Whisk in the olive oil and then the black beans. Let the vinaigrette sit for at least 2 hours, preferably overnight.

To Serve

Cut the ends of the spring rolls flat then cut the rolls in half, and cut each half in half again, this time cutting on a diagonal. Toss the arugula with the vinaigrette and arrange on plates. Stand 5 of the crab rolls on end around the arugula. Garnish with New York popcorn shoots.

GLAZED CHICKEN BREAST WITH MESCLUN AND DAIKON RADISH
(Serves 4)

4   skinless chicken breasts

MUSTARD GLAZE

$1/4$ cup dry mustard powder

$1/4$ cup sugar

$1/4$ cup soy sauce

This glaze is best made the day before. Stir the mustard and sugar together then whisk in the soy sauce. Preheat the oven to 400°F. Sauté the chicken breasts until golden (approximately 4 minutes), then brush on the soy glaze and bake in a hot oven until breasts are cooked (approximately 7 minutes). Let the chicken cool to room temperature and then slice it thinly lengthwise to get long slices.

VINAIGRETTE

$1/4$ cup brown rice vinegar

1   Tbs. sugar

1   Tbs. salt

3   tsp. soy sauce

3   tsp. ginger juice

$^3/_4$ cup extra virgin olive oil

To make the ginger juice, grate the ginger, then press it in a fine sieve or through cheesecloth. Whisk together the first 5 ingredients then whisk in the olive oil. Taste and adjust seasoning.

PICKLED DAIKON AND CARROT CURL GARNISH

1 cup rice vinegar

2 Tbs. sugar

1 Tbs. salt

1 med. carrot, cut into curls on a mandoline

1 med. daikon radish, cut into curls on a mandoline

4 cups lightly packed mesclun, washed and dried

2 Tbs. toasted black and white sesame seeds

Heat the vinegar, sugar, and salt together until the sugar and salt dissolve. Remove from heat and set aside to cool. When this mixture is cool, toss it with the radish and carrot separately and let the vegetables sit for 10 minutes to pickle.

To Serve

Dress the greens lightly with the vinaigrette. Pile greens in the center of each plate. Fan the chicken slices and balance the chicken against the greens; garnish with pickled daikon and carrot curls, then sprinkle black and white sesame seeds over all.

SPICE-CRUSTED PORK TENDERLOIN WITH DAIKON RADISH

(Serves 4)

SPICE-CRUSTED PORK TENDERLOIN

2 pork tenderloins, trimmed of fat and silverskin (this can be done by your butcher)

2 Tbs. ground cumin

$^1/_2$ tsp. ground cinnamon

3 Tbs. peanut oil

1 tsp. freshly ground pepper

Salt to taste

PHOTO: *Spice-crusted pork tenderloin with daikon radish*

Preheat oven to 450°F. Mix the cumin, cinnamon, and ground pepper. Season the pork tenderloins with salt, then roll them in the spice powder mix and sauté in peanut oil in a hot pan over medium heat; cook on each side for 1 minute. Finish cooking in the oven until the pork is medium rare (approximately 7 minutes). Let the pork rest for 10 minutes.

DAIKON ROOT WITH CUMIN AND TURMERIC

1 lg. daikon root, peeled and cut into bite-size chunks

1 Tbs. ground turmeric

1 Tbs. ground cumin

1 cup light chicken stock

Salt and pepper to taste

Simmer the daikon root with the spices, salt, pepper, and chicken stock in a covered pot over a low flame. Stir occasionally to make sure the daikon cooks evenly.

SNOW PEAS

$^1/_2$ lb. snow peas, trimmed and cut into thirds on an angle

1 Tbs. butter

Salt and pepper to taste

Steam the snow peas and toss with butter, salt, and pepper.

To Serve
Pile the daikon chunks in the middle of the plate. Slice the pork tenderloin and fan at the front of the daikon. Scatter the snow peas around the plate and serve immediately.

SAKE-POACHED COD WITH QUINOA AND SHIITAKES
(Serves 4)

QUINOA WITH SHIITAKE MUSHROOMS
1   cup quinoa, rinsed until the rinsing water runs clear
$1/4$ oz. dried shiitake mushrooms ($1/2$ cup if using dried sliced mushrooms, 4 caps if using dried whole caps)
2   cups water
2   teaspoons salt
1   medium carrot, cut across the center into threads on a mandoline

To toast the rinsed quinoa, stir it in a dry 2-quart saucepan over medium heat until it is dry and a little darker. It should smell pleasantly nutty. Add 2 cups of boiling water with the salt and dried mushrooms. Be careful as the water will splatter as it hits the hot pan bottom. Let the quinoa come to a boil, then cover and let it simmer for 15 minutes. Quickly add the carrot threads to the pot then cover again. Remove the pot from the heat and let rest for 7 minutes, then fluff with a fork.

SAKE POACHED COD
$1^1/2$ lb. of cod fillet, preferably cut from the thick end of the fish, cut into 4 pieces
3   cups sake
2   branches celery, cut into $1/2$-inch lengths
2   bay leaves
2   branches fresh thyme
2   Tbs. flat leaf parsley leaves, washed and julienned

Heat the sake, celery, bay leaves, thyme, and salt in a shallow pan. Add the cod and reduce heat to low. Cover the pan and let simmer until the cod turns opaque (about 9 minutes). Mix $1/2$ cup of the hot cooking liquid with the julienned parsley.

To Serve
Pile quinoa in the center of each warmed plate. Arrange a piece of cod on the side of each pile. Spoon 2 tablespoons of the parsley liquid over the fish and serve.

WARM WINTER FRUIT COMPOTE OF QUINCE, PRUNES, AND APRICOTS SOAKED IN EARL GREY TEA AND ORANGES
(Serves 4)

DRIED FRUIT WITH EARL GREY TEA
8   pitted prunes

WINE

The Aroma Wheel

The Aroma Wheel is useful when describing wines. It was developed at the University of California at Davis by professor Ann Noble. She took wine makers' descriptions of wines, terms like apricot, cherry, berry, et cetera, and, being a food scientist, got the same fruits and analyzed the components of the two. She found that wines and the fruits used to describe them had the exact same molecular structure or compounds. Start in the center of the Wheel and ask yourself: What does this wine smell like? If it smells fruity, then go to the next layer. What kind of fruit? Is it a tree fruit? Once you have identified what type of fruit go to the next level. These decriptions help in discussing wines.

8   whole dried apricots

2   cups water that has just come to the boiling point

3   Tbs. Earl Grey tea

Pour the boiling water over the tea and let steep for 4 minutes. Strain the tea off the leaves and soak the dried fruits separately in hot tea. Let fruit stand for at least $1/2$ hour at room temperature or overnight in the refrigerator.

SPICED QUINCE

1   cup sugar

2   cups water

1   stick of cinnamon

$1/2$ Tbs. whole clove

4   whole peppercorns

$1/2$ lemon, juiced

$1/2$ orange, juiced

2    $1/4$-inch slices fresh ginger

3   medium quince, peeled and cut into bite-size pieces

2   lg. seedless oranges, cut into segments

2   blood oranges, cut into segments

Place the clove, peppercorns, lemon and orange juice, and ginger in a saucepan and bring to a boil to dissolve the sugar. Quince oxidizes very quickly, so work on 1 quince at a time. Peel the quince and cut into bite-size pieces. Place in the poaching liquid immediately, and poach with a sheet of parchment paper pressed to the surface until the quince are soft.

To Serve

Let the orange segments macerate in the quince liquid for 15 minutes, then assemble the plates. Arrange the quince, rehydrated dried fruit, and oranges in dessert bowls and add quince cooking liquid to moisten. Serve warm.

STYLE

A Slightly Asian Mood

The Zen school of thought seeks to escape slavery to words and logic. So, to heighten our senses, we create a slightly Asian mood with items gathered from the mystic East:

- Tea boxes and puzzles decorate our sideboard.
- A bonsai plant rests on a hunter green napkin mat.
- Bamboo place mats are functional and add fun and texture to the table top.
- Blue-stemmed glassware lends a shock of cobalt color.
- Blue ceramic plates with an intricate Asian motif and matching cups and saucers give character to the table.
- Something as simple as a fanned napkin can add grace and beauty.
- The flicker of a candle through glass is romantic and enticing.
- Matching guests, meals, and chopsticks makes for great fun.

BERNARD GUILLAS

LA JOLLA BEACH & TENNIS CLUB, INC.
LA JOLLA, CALIFORNIA.

APPETIZERS

MINESTRONE

PETALS OF FRESH SEA SCAL-
LOPS CARPACCIO STYLE WITH
EXOTIC FRUIT RELISH, LIME,
SESAME OIL, AND CHIVES

MARINE ROOM MAINE LOBSTER
BISQUE WITH SHIITAKE MUSH-
ROOMS, CHIVES, AND ROASTED
SUNFLOWER SEEDS

ENTRÉES

OVEN-ROASTED MALLARD DUCK
BREAST WITH PECAN-FIG RISOT-
TO AND FONDUE OF BERMUDA
ONION, SHIITAKE MUSHROOMS,
AND TARRAGON

SEARED FRESH FILET OF SEA
BASS WITH LEMON-THYME
HOISIN SAUCE AND MACADAMIA-
PEANUT CRUST SERVED ATOP A
RED LENTIL SALSA, SAFFRON
MARJORAM CHARDONNAY SAUCE

DESSERT

"PRIDE OF LA JOLLA" HONEY-
GOLDEN NEST OF SUMMER SOR-
BET TRIO, CINNAMON DUSTED
AND SERVED WITH SPICY WILD
BERRY PURÉE

"A good cook is like a sorcerer who dispenses happiness on a plate," exclaims the Executive Chef de Cuisine of the La Jolla Beach & Tennis Club, Inc., in La Jolla, California. Chef Guillas oversees all menus and wine lists for the La Jolla Beach and Tennis Club, the Sea Lodge hotel, and the historic landmark Marine Room restaurant.

Born in Brittany, France, to a family of butchers, bakers, and restaurateurs, Chef Guillas received his formal training under the legendary Georges Paineau at La Bretagne in Questembert, France. Guillas spent the next six years honing his culinary acumen as an apprentice and Sous Chef at L'Abbaye de Villeneuve and L'Auberge Normande in France, where he added pastry and pantry expertise. Next, Guillas moved to French Guiana in South America where he accepted the position of manager and Chef de Cuisine at Le Dolmen; this experience was a source of the diverse flavors that influence his palate today. Chef Guillas returned to France to work as Sous Chef at Les Maraichers to strengthen his management skills. He then moved to Washington, D.C. in 1984, working for three celebrated years at Maison Blanche under the direction of Pierre Chambrin. In 1987, Chef Guillas left Maison Blanche to work as Sous Chef at the Nicholas Restaurant in the Mayflower Hotel.

Two years later Guillas moved to San Diego to work at the Grant Grill, where he received numerous honors and accolades. The San Diego Restaurant Association gave its top honor, the Gold Medallion, to Chef Guillas at the Grant Grill from 1991 through 1994 for best hotel restaurant. He was awarded the Golden Platter by the International Food, Wine & Travel Writers Association in 1990 and *The Wine Spectator*'s Award of Excellence from 1990 through 1992.

PHOTO: *Oven-roasted Mallard duck breast with pecan-fig risotto and fondue of Bermuda onion, shiitake mushrooms, and tarragon*

MINESTRONE
(Serves 6)

MINESTRONE

1	Tbs. olive oil
1/4	cup onions, chopped
1/4	cup celery, finely diced
1	cup leeks, sliced
1	cup fava beans
1	cup corn
1	cup cherry tomatoes, cut in half
1	cup yellow and red teardrop tomatoes, cut in half
1	Tbs. garlic, diced
1	Tbs. basil, chopped
1	tsp. lemon thyme
1	tsp. chicken base or 1 bouillon cube
1	qt. water

Sauté all ingredients in olive oil in a hot stock pot over medium heat for 2 minutes. Deglaze with water and simmer for 20 minutes.

GARNISH

12	basil leaves, cut into a chiffonade
1	sundried tomato herb baguette

Cut baguette into thin slices and toast. Set aside for service.

To Serve
Ladle soup into a bowl and float a toasted baguette crouton in the center. Sprinkle basil chiffonade over the top and serve.

PHOTO: *Petals of fresh sea scallops carpaccio style with exotic fruit relish, lime, sesame oil, and chives*

PETALS OF FRESH SEA SCALLOPS CARPACCIO STYLE WITH EXOTIC FRUIT RELISH, LIME, SESAME OIL, AND CHIVES
(Serves 6)

EXOTIC FRUIT RELISH

1	papaya, minced
6	lychees, minced
1	mango, minced
1	kiwi, diced
1	tsp. ginger, grated
2	Tbs. peach schnapps

In a large bowl, mix fruits with grated ginger and peach schnapps. Set aside for 30 minutes.

SEA SCALLOPS

12 jumbo fresh sea scallops (substitute salmon or
    sea bass)
3 limes, juiced
2 Tbs. chives, finely chopped
2 Tbs. light sesame oil
2 Tbs. parmesan cheese, freshly grated
Salt and pepper to taste

Cut each scallop horizontally into 5 slices and set aside.

GARNISH

18 basil leaves
6 chive blossoms
1 tsp. paprika

To Serve

Place 2 tablespoons of fruit relish in the center of a plate and
arrange raw sea scallops as petals around the relish creating a
flower (the center being fruit relish).

Delicately drizzle each sea scallop with lime juice and
sesame oil and season with salt and pepper. Then sprinkle with
parmesan cheese and chives. Garnish each "flower" with a
chive blossom and 3 basil leaves. Dust edges of the plate with
paprika and serve.

MARINE ROOM MAINE LOBSTER BISQUE WITH SHIITAKE MUSHROOMS, CHIVES, AND ROASTED SUNFLOWER SEEDS

(Serves 6 to 8)

LOBSTER BISQUE

$1/4$ cup olive oil
2 lb. lobster shells, chopped
1 celery stalk, chopped
1 white onion, chopped
1 small leek, chopped
1 garlic clove
$1/4$ cup apricot brandy
$1/3$ cup tomato paste

2 Tbs. flour
$1/2$ cup white wine
1 pt. fish stock
1 qt. water
1 tsp. lobster base
1 bay leaf
2 fresh tomatoes, diced
1 tsp. tarragon, chopped
2 Tbs. apricot brandy
$3/4$ cup heavy cream
1 2-lb. Maine lobster, steamed, shelled, and cut into
    1-inch pieces
Pinch of cayenne pepper, to taste

In a large soup pan, sauté chopped lobster shells with olive oil
at high heat, then add the celery, onions, leeks, and garlic,
cooking for approximately 10 minutes. Flambé with 2 tablespoons of apricot brandy and incorporate tomato paste and
flour, mixing well with a wooden spatula. Allow to cook for 2
minutes, then add white wine, fish stock, water, lobster base,
bay leaf, and diced tomato. Stir and simmer at medium heat
for approximately 45 minutes.

Strain soup through a sieve, pressing shells to extract
maximum amount of pulp and liquid. Return soup to a large
pot and bring to a boil, then add the heavy cream and continue to cook for approximately 5 minutes. Season with salt, 2
tablespoons of apricot brandy, and cayenne pepper.

GARNISH

1 Tbs. chives, finely chopped
6 med. shiitake mushrooms, stemmed, sliced, and
    sautéed
1 Tbs. roasted sunflower seeds

To Serve

Place sautéed shiitake mushrooms in bottom of soup plate,
pour in lobster bisque, and garnish with lobster medallions,
chives, and roasted sunflower seeds. Serve hot.

OVEN-ROASTED MALLARD DUCK BREAST WITH PECAN-FIG RISOTTO AND FONDUE OF BERMUDA ONION, SHIITAKE MUSH-ROOMS, AND TARRAGON

(Serves 6)

OVEN-ROASTED MALLARD DUCK BREAST

2	mallard duck breasts, fat side scored
2	Tbs. olive oil
1/2	cup orange juice
2	Tbs. balsamic vinegar
3	Tbs. teriyaki sauce
1/4	cup chicken stock
1	Tbs. shallots, chopped
1	Tbs. butter
1	Tbs. opal basil, chopped
1/2	tsp. corn starch, diluted with 1 Tbs. of water
	Salt and pepper to taste

Preheat oven to 400°F degrees. Season duck breast with salt and pepper. In a hot skillet, sear breast, skin-side up, for approximately 2 minutes; turn breasts over and place in the preheated oven. Cook for approximately 10 minutes. Remove and set aside. Degrease pan and add shallots; cook until translucent. Deglaze with orange juice, balsamic vinegar, and teriyaki; reduce by half. Add chicken stock and reduce by half again. Add corn starch mixture. Whisk in butter until fully incorporated. Finish with chopped opal basil and season to taste.

FONDUE OF BERMUDA ONION, SHIITAKE MUSHROOMS, AND TARRAGON

1	cup Bermuda onion, sliced
2	Tbs. brown sugar
2	limes, juiced
1	cup shiitake mushrooms, sliced
1	tsp. tarragon, chopped
2	Tbs. sweet butter
1	Tbs. chile oil
	Salt and pepper to taste

In a saucepan over medium heat, melt butter. Add onions and sauté for 1 minute. Add brown sugar and cook until fully dissolved; do not allow to caramelize. Add shiitake mushrooms and cook for another minute. Deglaze saucepan with lime juice and chile oil and cook at medium heat until liquid has evaporated. Season with salt and pepper.

PECAN-FIG RISOTTO

4	Tbs. butter
1/2	cup scallions, minced
1/2	cup Arborio rice
2	cups chicken stock
1/4	cup dried figs, quartered
1/3	cup pecans
	Salt and pepper to taste

In a saucepan over medium heat, melt 3 tablespoons of butter and add minced scallions. Cook for approximately 2 minutes. Add rice and stir for 1 minute. Pour in chicken stock and bring to a boil. Cover and cook on low heat for approximately 30 minutes, stirring frequently. Stir in remaining butter with pecans and dried figs. Continue to cook at low heat for another 5 minutes uncovered. Season to taste.

GARNISH

4	sprigs opal basil
4	fresh figs

To Serve

Place onion fondue around center of serving plate creating a bed, then place a "molded" risotto rice cup in the center of plate atop the fondue (fill a small cup and pat down the risotto, turn upside-down and remove cup carefully). Remove fat from duck breast and slice thin. Create a crown with the sliced duck around risotto rice cup (slices all standing). Gently ladle sauce over the crown and garnish with opal basil sprigs and fresh figs. Serve hot.

Wine Recommendation

Ivan Tamas Reserve Cabernet Sauvignon

SEARED FRESH FILET OF SEA BASS WITH LEMON-THYME HOISIN SAUCE AND MACADAMIA-PEANUT CRUST, SERVED ATOP A RED LENTIL SALSA, SAFFRON MARJORAM CHARDONNAY SAUCE

(Serves 6)

MACADAMIA-PEANUT CRUST

3	oz. macadamia nuts, ground
3	oz. peanuts, ground
2	oz. Hoisin sauce
1	tsp. lemon-thyme, chopped
2	Tbs. orange juice
1	Tbs. lime juice
1	Tbs. honey

Mix ground nuts and set aside. Mix Hoisin sauce with lemon-thyme, orange juice, lime juice, and honey. Set aside.

SEA BASS

6	7-oz. white sea bass filets, skinned and boned
2	oz. olive oil
	Salt and pepper to taste

Preheat oven to 400°F. Rub filets with olive oil and season with salt and pepper; refrigerate while preparing the rest of the dish. Coat the bottom of a skillet with olive oil at medium heat. Once oil is hot, place the filet in the skillet and sear for approximately 2 minutes. Turn over and baste with Hoisin sauce mix, then sprinkle to cover filets with the peanut-macadamia nut mix. Place in oven and cook for approximately 12 minutes. Remove fish when golden brown.

RED LENTIL SALSA

4	cups water
2	cups red lentils
2	Tbs. cilantro, chopped
1	cup tomato, diced
2	Tbs. mint, chopped
1	Tbs. hazelnut oil
	Dash Tabasco

Salt and pepper to taste

In a saucepan, bring 4 cups of water to a boil and cook red lentils for approximately 10 minutes. Remove and rinse under cold water. Strain the lentils and add scallions, tomatoes, mint, hazelnut oil, Tabasco, salt, and pepper. Set aside.

SAFFRON MARJORAM CHARDONNAY SAUCE

1	shallot, minced
1	cup chardonnay
1/4	cup white wine vinegar
1	tsp. marjoram, chopped
2	sticks of sweet butter, sliced
	Pinch saffron threads
	Salt and pepper to taste

Reduce chardonnay, shallots, saffron, and vinegar together by half. Whisk in slices of butter until fully incorporated. Season to taste with salt, pepper, and marjoram.

GARNISH

6	mint sprigs
6	lemon crowns

To Serve

Divide red lentil salsa among 6 serving plates, then place sea bass filet atop each. Ladle out the sauce, building a ledge around the filet. Garnish each plate with a fresh mint sprig and a lemon crown.

"PRIDE OF LA JOLLA" HONEY GOLDEN NEST OF SUMMER SORBET TRIO, CINNAMON DUSTED AND SERVED WITH SPICY WILD BERRY PUREE

(Serves 6 to 8)

PASSION FRUIT SORBET

1	cup water
1	cup sugar
1/4	cup white wine

$^3/_4$ cup pulp scooped from halved ripe passion fruits

$^1/_2$ cup orange juice

2 Tbs. aged tequila

Stir together the water, sugar, and wine in a small saucepan and bring to a boil over medium heat. Remove and allow to cool at room temperature. In a food processor, purée the passion fruit pulp with the orange juice. Strain and remove seeds (save 1 tablespoon).

Stir together the syrup, fruit purée, reserved seeds, and tequila. Process in an ice cream machine or sorbet maker. Transfer to a plastic container with a lid and freeze.

PINK GRAPEFRUIT SORBET

1 cup water

1 cup sugar

$^1/_4$ cup white wine

$1^1/_4$ cups pink grapefruit juice

2 Tbs. white tequila

Stir together the water, sugar, and wine in a small saucepan and bring to a boil over medium heat. Remove and allow to cool at room temperature.

Stir together the syrup, grapefruit juice, and tequila. Process in an ice cream machine or sorbet maker. Transfer to a plastic container with a lid and freeze.

CACTUS PEAR SORBET

1 cup water

1 cup sugar

$^1/_4$ cup white wine

1 lb. ripe cactus pears, peeled (be careful with the spines)

2 Tbs. lime juice

Stir together the water, sugar, and wine in small saucepan and

WINE

Making a Great Wine

Grapes are usually harvested in the coastal valleys of California starting in September. As the grapes come into the winery they are pressed to remove the juice. The grapes are pressed as gently as possible to avoid getting solids or a smashing of grapes that imparts bitterness. To the one hundred percent grape juice, only yeast is added, which eats the sugar in the juice as its food source, and converts it to alcohol, releasing carbon dioxide into the atmosphere. If the yeast consumes all the sugar, turning it to alcohol, the wine will not be sweet but dry. For a slightly sweet wine, the fermentation is stopped before the yeast has eaten all the natural grape sugar.

After the fermentation process, many wines, both white and red, will go into barrels to be aged. The barrels impart a flavor and complexity to the wine caused by the extract from the oak and oxidation of the wines as they breath through the porous wood barrel. This process mellows wines. After aging, the wine is filtered, bottled and sent to market.

bring to a boil over medium heat. Remove and allow to cool at room temperature.

In a food processor, purée the cactus pear. Strain, measure 1¼ cup of juice, and set aside. Stir together syrup, cactus pear juice, and lime juice. Process in an ice cream machine or sorbet maker. Transfer to a plastic container with a lid and freeze.

WILD BERRY PUREE

²/₃	cup fresh blackberries and raspberries, finely chopped
4	Tbs. sugar
1	Tbs. tequila
2	tsp. cilantro, finely chopped
½	tsp. mint, finely chopped
½	tsp. small jalapeño chili, seeded and finely chopped
1	tsp. lime juice

Stir together all ingredients and refrigerate in a covered container.

GOLDEN LUMPIA CHIPS

2½	Tbs. honey
6	4-inch Lumpia dough sheets
2	Tbs. confectioners' sugar
1	tsp. cinnamon
6	cilantro sprigs (garnish)

Heat 4 inches of canola oil in a tall heavy pan or deep fryer to approximately 350°F. In a small saucepan, gently warm honey over low heat until liquid. Using a small stainless steel ladle to hold lumpias under oil to form a tulip shape, fry lumpias one at a time until golden brown. Drain on paper towels. Lightly brush golden lumpias with honey. Dust each "tulip" with a mixture of sugar and cinnamon.

Place a tulip on each serving plate. Place a small scoop of each sorbet (1½ oz. each) in each tulip. Spoon 3 tablespoons wild berry purée around the tulip on each plate. Garnish with cilantro sprigs and serve.

STYLE

Some Enchanted Evening

For that special holiday or celebrating a promotion, winning the lottery, or selling that first novel, an enchanted evening begins with style and ends with great food.

On a simple white tablecloth, place a gold underplate called a charger. Upon that, place beautiful gold band and star plates to reflect the honored guest. Gold flatware complements the plates and chargers, and gold-banded stemware con-

tinues the motif. Grapes on a charger make a simple but elegant centerpiece and a great accompaniment to dessert cheeses, fruits, and cookies. Take care that the acid In the fruit does not discolor the charger. Continue the star theme with napkin rings and magically festive gold baskets for your guests to take home along with cherished memories.

CRAIG HENNE

TARRYTOWN HOUSE CONFERENCE CENTER
TARRYTOWN, NEW YORK

APPETIZERS

MOREL-CRUSTED VEAL CARPAC-
CIO WITH WARM FLAKED TUNA
AND CAPER DRESSING

ENTRÉES

PANZEROTTI FILLED WITH
BROCCOLI RABE AND RICOTTA
CHEESE WITH OVEN-ROASTED
TOMATO SAUCE

ANGUS BEEF TENDERLOIN WITH
HERB CRUST IN PORCINI
MUSHROOM RAGOUT

GRILLED AHI TUNA IN A STEW
OF ROASTED PEPPERS AND
LENTILS, FENNEL GRATINE

DESSERTS

WARM FLOURLESS CHOCOLATE
TART, WHITE CHOCOLATE ICE
CREAM, AND FRESH MINT
SABAYON

Executive Chef Craig Henne took over all culinary operations at Tarrytown House in May 1996. Tarrytown House Conference Center is located in the lower Hudson Valley on twenty-six acres and is comprised of two estates, the Biddle Mansion and the King House.

Prior to joining the culinary force at Tarrytown House, Chef Henne held the position of Executive Chef at the Ritz-Carlton in New York for five years. His responsibilities included room service and banquets as well as overseeing all culinary operations of Fantino Restaurant. His dedication earned the restaurant the coveted American Automobile Association's (AAA) Five Diamond Award as well as Mobil's four-star rating. In addition, Fantino became one of the premier Italian restaurants in Manhattan, gaining a three-star rating from *Crain's New York Business* magazine. Chef Henne's culinary talents gained the restaurant further fame by earning it a place on *Esquire* magazine's list "Cheers! The Best New Restaurants of 1994."

Chef Henne is a graduate of the Culinary Institute of America in Hyde Park, New York, and he previously held the positions of Banquet Chef at the Helmsley Palace and Executive Chef of Trumpets restaurant at the Grand Hyatt, both in Manhattan.

PHOTO: *Angus beef tenderloin with herb crust in porcini mushroom ragout*

MOREL-CRUSTED VEAL CARPACCIO WITH WARM FLAKED TUNA AND CAPER DRESSING

(Serves 4)

MOREL-CRUSTED VEAL

12　oz. veal loin, trimmed
3　oz. dry morel mushrooms
1　oz. olive oil
Salt and pepper

Purée dry morel mushrooms in a food processor to finely chopped crumbs. Season raw, trimmed veal loin with salt and pepper. Roll veal in morel crumbs. Heat olive oil in sauté pan until hot. Sear morel-crusted veal loin in hot oil on all sides, just browning exterior (do not cook veal). Set aside to cool.

TUNA CAPER DRESSING

8　oz. tuna filet
1　oz. capers
1　lemon, juiced
4　oz. extra virgin olive oil
1　Tbs. parsley, chopped fine
Salt and pepper

Season tuna with salt and pepper and grill, keeping it very rare. Transfer to a plate. Using a fork, push down on tuna and flake it apart. In a sauté pan, heat olive oil until warm. Add capers and lemon juice and stir. Next add flaked tuna, chopped parsley, salt, and pepper, being careful not to cook tuna.

BABY GREENS

1　cup baby arugula
2　oz. Parmigiana cheese, shaved

To Serve
Place 5 overlapping slices of veal on each plate, creating a cir-cle. Place baby arugula and shaved Parmigiana cheese slices in center of plate. After the above is done, heat tuna dressing. Portion dressing and spoon over veal slices. Serve immediately.

PANZEROTTI FILLED WITH BROCCOLI RABE AND RICOTTA CHEESE WITH OVEN-ROASTED TOMATO SAUCE

(Serves 4)

BROCCOLI RABE

2　bunches broccoli rabe
8　oz. ricotta cheese
2　Tbs. Parmesan cheese
2　cloves garlic
1　pinch crushed red pepper
Salt to taste
1　oz. extra virgin olive oil

Trim outer leaves and tough stems of broccoli rabe. Blanch in salted boiling water until soft (not al dente). Shock in ice water and squeeze out all moisture. In a sauté pan over medium heat, roast garlic cloves in olive oil. Once roasted, add blanched broc-coli rabe and sauté. Remove from pan and let cool. Place all remaining ingredients in a food processor with sautéed broccoli rabe and purée until smooth. Check seasoning.

PASTA DOUGH

4　oz. unbleached all-purpose flour
4　oz. Durham flour
1　tsp. salt
1　tsp. olive oil
4　whole eggs
Egg wash

Combine both flours on a counter top and form a well. Add remaining ingredients and knead together until it forms a dough. Roll through a pasta machine into very thin sheets. Allow sheets to dry but still to be pliable. Using a cutter 4 inches in diameter, cut out 16 circles. Place 2 tablespoons of broccoli rabe mixture in the center of each circle. Egg wash the

PHOTO: *Morel-crusted veal carpaccio with warm flaked tuna and caper dressing*

perimeter. Pinch pasta closed, creating a half-moon shape ravioli. Using both hands, place ravioli tips between thumb and index finger. Pinch pasta and push inward, creating a Napoleon hat shape. Place down and let rest. The pasta may be stored in a freezer until ready to cook.

To cook Panzerotti, place in a pot with salted boiling water and cook for 7 minutes. Remove from water and place in a sauté pan with 2 ounces of olive oil. Sauté gently over medium heat. Finish in sauté pan with 2 ounces grated Parmigiana cheese, coating Panzerotti well.

OVEN-ROASTED TOMATO SAUCE

16	ripe plum tomatoes
1	bunch fresh basil, cleaned and chopped
2	garlic cloves
1	Tbs. fresh thyme, chopped
6	oz. olive oil

Slice stem end off plum tomatoes and quarter tomatoes lengthwise. In a blender, purée basil, thyme, garlic, and olive oil. Toss the mixture in a bowl with quartered tomatoes. Once well tossed, place tomatoes on a sheet pan covered with a rack.

Place in an oven at 150 to 200°F. Let dry in oven for 2 to 4 hours. Remove when tomatoes are fully dried and roasted.

1   Tbs. basil, chiffonade
4   oz. extra virgin olive oil
Salt and white pepper to taste

Place oven-roasted tomatoes and basil chiffonade in a food processor and purée while slowly adding virgin olive oil. When chunky, and olive oil is incorporated, remove from food processor. Heat in a sauté pan and adjust seasoning. Sauce should be thick.

To Serve

Spoon hot oven-roasted tomato sauce in center of pasta bowls. Stand 4 broccoli rabe Panzerottis on top of tomato sauce. Garnish with basil sprigs and Parmigiana cheese.

ANGUS BEEF TENDERLOIN WITH HERB CRUST IN PORCINI MUSHROOM RAGOUT
(Serves 4)

BEEF TENDERLOIN

4   6-oz. angus beef filets
3   Tbs. vegetable oil
Salt and black pepper

Season beef filets with salt and black pepper. In a sauté pan using the vegetable oil, sear the filets over a high flame. Turn the filets over and caramelize on both sides.

HERB CRUST

3/4   lb. parsley root (parsnips), peeled
1   lb. butter
1   lb. white bread crumbs (fresh, no crust)
1   clove garlic
1   bunch parsley
2   oz. basil
2   oz. tarragon
2   oz. thyme
1   lemon, juice only
3   egg yolks
Salt and pepper to taste

Cut parsley root into small pieces. Cook in salted water with the juice of 1 lemon. When soft, strain and push through a sieve. Blanch herbs in salted water and shock in an ice bath to stop the cooking process.

Whip room-temperature butter until smooth. Add parsley root, white bread, egg yolks, and chopped garlic. Purée herbs in blender and add to butter mixture. Season with salt and pepper. Roll finished herb crust into silver-dollar-sized rolls and wrap in plastic wrap. This recipe will yield more than 4 servings, so place in freezer for future use.

PORCINI MUSHROOM RAGOUT

12   oz. porcini mushrooms, fresh or frozen
6   oz. madeira wine
16   oz. veal jus
1   shallot, finely diced
1   oz. butter, clarified

In a sauce pot, sauté diced shallots and sliced porcini mushrooms in clarified butter. Once tender, deglaze pot with madeira wine and reduce to 3/4. Then add veal jus and reduce by half or until desired thickness. Season with salt and pepper. Keep warm.

To Serve

Using a French knife, cut 1-inch-thick slices of herb crust and place over each seared beef filet. Place in 350°F preheated oven and cook until desired doneness and herb crust has slightly browned. Spoon the mushroom porcini ragout in center of each plate and top with herb-crusted beef tenderloin. Serve immediately.

GRILLED AHI TUNA IN A STEW OF ROASTED PEPPERS AND LENTILS, FENNEL GRATINE

(Serves 4)

TUNA LOIN

4	6 to 7 oz. tuna steaks
1	oz. extra virgin olive oil
	Salt and pepper

Season tuna with salt and pepper. Roll in olive oil and grill to desired doneness.

LENTILS

12	oz. dried brown lentils
1	white onion, diced fine
1	oz. prosciutto
28	oz. vegetable stock
1	roasted red pepper, diced fine
1	roasted yellow pepper, diced fine

BOUQUET GARNI

3	sprigs rosemary
2	sprigs thyme
1	bay leaf
	Salt and pepper

To roast the peppers, wash and dry well and place on gas range top over an open flame until the skin is charred black. If a gas range top is not available, the same result may be obtained by using the broiler in the oven; this, however, will take longer to achieve the desired result. Once the skin is thoroughly charred, remove the pepper from the heat and place in an ice bath to stop the cooking process. Under running water, peel away all of the charred skin from the pepper; what is left is the delicious roasted-flavored meat of the pepper.

In a heavy-bottomed saucepan, render proscuitto over low flame. Once rendered, add fine-diced onions and sauté until translucent. Add lentils and coat with rendered proscuitto. Add bouquet garni and vegetable stock. Simmer lentils until tender, reducing liquid until lentils are thick. Finish lentils with finely-diced roasted peppers, season with salt and pepper. Keep warm.

FENNEL GRATINE

1	fennel head
12	oz. water
2	oz. all-purpose flour
3	oz. Parmigiana cheese, grated fine
1	Tbs. rosemary-infused olive oil

Bring water and salt to a boil. Whisk in flour, making a blanche. Cook trimmed fennel head in blanche until tender. Set aside and let cool. Cut fennel heads in half, removing inner leaves and heart. Slice fennel into julienne strips. Toss cooked julienne fennel in a bowl with Parmigiana cheese and vegetable stock from lentils and season with salt and pepper.

To Serve

Place fennel gratine mix on top of each cooked tuna steak and lightly brown under a broiler. While this is browning, spoon lentil and roasted pepper stew in center of each plate. Top lentils with tuna and fennel gratine. Drizzle plate with rosemary-infused olive oil.

WARM FLOURLESS CHOCOLATE TART, WHITE CHOCOLATE ICE CREAM, AND FRESH MINT SABAYON

(Serves 4)

CHOCOLATE TART

12	oz. butter
10	oz. bittersweet chocolate
7	egg yolks
3	oz. sugar
1	oz. Kahlua
7	egg whites
1	tsp. salt

Preheat oven to 450°F. Melt butter and chocolate together over a water bath. Mix together the egg yolks, sugar, and Kahlua. Fold butter-chocolate mix into yolk mix. Whip egg whites and salt together into a meringue (stiff peaks but not dry). Fold meringue into chocolate mixture until completely incorporated. Place mixture in the preheated oven for 3 minutes exactly. Remove and set aside to cool.

PASTRY SHEETS

4   chocolate puff pastry sheets (plain puff pastry when only available)

4   5-inch tart shells

1   lb. dried beans, any kind

WINE

Aging Wine in Barrels

Some wine ages in barrels made of oak, which comes from all over the world. A combination of American, French, Yugoslavian, and Moravian oak is used in American wineries. As the American wine industry matures, more technical research is being done to better understand the wonderful flavors that each different oak from around the world imparts to the wine. Many barrel makers actually char the inside of the barrel, giving it a light, medium, or heavy toasting. This imparts a smoky character to the wine that can be quite pleasant.

A rich, oaky flavor adds to the enjoyment of wine, but should be balanced and not overpowering. Red wines, richer in tannins, make a great accompaniment to beef, lamb, and other red meats.

2   sheets wax paper

Roll out puff pastry dough to 1/8-inch thickness and line individual tart shells. Top puff pastry with wax paper covered with dried beans (for weight only). Cook tart shells weighed down in a 350°F oven until cooked through and crisp, approximately 10 to 15 minutes. Remove wax paper and beans. Fill tarts with chocolate mix and bake in a 450°F oven for 3 minutes. Remove tarts from oven and set aside to cool.

WHITE CHOCOLATE ICE CREAM

16   oz. milk

6   oz. sugar

6–8 egg yolks

4   oz. white chocolate

In a heavy-bottomed sauce pot, scald milk. In a bowl, mix egg yolks and sugar. Slowly add milk to egg yolk and sugar mix. Once well combined, pour mix back into the sauce pot. Stir continuously over medium heat until mixture can coat the back of a spoon. While this mix is cooking, melt chocolate over a water bath. Pour milk and egg mix into melted chocolate and whisk. When well incorporated, set aside to cool down. Freeze in an ice cream maker.

MINT SABAYON

4   egg yolks

3   oz. sugar

2   oz. crème de menthe

Combine egg yolks and sugar in a bowl and whip over a water bath until thick. Remove from heat, add the crème de menthe, and whip the sabayon at room temperature until mix forms ribbons. Set aside for garnish.

To Serve

Place filled tart shells in 450°F oven and bake for approximately 3 minutes. Remove when the centers are still wet and place in center of plate. Top tarts with an oval-shaped scoop of white chocolate ice cream. Spoon mint Sabayon over ice cream and serve.

STYLE

A Study in Black and White

A black tablecloth forms the foundation on which to place black-and-white-checked oversized placemats.

Stark white plates frame your culinary creations and add to the art of the tabletop.

The black stems of the wineglasses continue the theme.

Table accessories hold bottles of water or wine, and breads, oils, and cheese become part of a simple table still life caught in the flicker of candles.

On the sideboard, flowers, candles, and vegetables carry the same theme and the promise of dessert.

DAVID HOLBEN

MEDITERRANEO
DALLAS, TEXAS

"Food from the heart," is how David Holben, Executive Chef and General Manager of Mediterraneo, describes his cooking. He developed his love for cooking in his mother's kitchen and also in the kitchen of Shaw's Restaurant in Lancaster, Ohio.

In 1980, after graduating with high honors from the Culinary Institute of America in Hyde Park, New York, Chef Holben moved to Dallas, Texas, to help Executive Chef Peter Schaffrath open Cafe Royale in the Plaza of the Americas Hotel. Three years later, Chef Holben received a one-year scholarship to further hone his skills with some of the most recognized chefs in France. He cooked alongside Roger Verge in the kitchens of Le Moulin de Mougin, L'Amandier, and Paul Bocuse in Lyon and L'Hôtel George V in Paris.

In 1984, Chef Holben returned to Dallas to work with restauranteur Franco Bertolasi in opening the longest-lasting five-star restaurant in Dallas, the Riviera. After ten years as Executive Chef of the critically acclaimed Riviera, Chef Holben and Franco Bertolasi opened Mediterraneo, which quickly became a four-star restaurant. In the tradition of the Riviera, the menu is inspired by the flavors of southern France and northern Italy. Toscana, their new venture, will feature contemporary Tuscan cuisine in an exciting, elegant atmosphere.

Chef Holben's awards and honors, however, do not end with his scholarship to study in France. In 1990, he was the recipient of *Food & Wine* magazine's Mumm's Cuvée Napa Award as one of the top ten best new chefs in the United States. The following year *Esquire* magazine's John Marianni said, "The Riviera is the best restaurant in Dallas and David Holben is the reason why." The *Zagat Guide* also rated Holben's food number one for the past five years.

PHOTO: *Grilled vegetable sandwich with new potato salad*

CRISPY SESAME LAVOSH PIZZA WITH APPLE-ONION MARMALADE, OVEN-DRIED TOMATOES, CALAMATA OLIVES, AND HERB GOAT CHEESE

(Serves 4)

SESAME LAVOSH

2 $1/3$ cups all purpose flour

2   Tbs. sugar

$1/2$ Tbs. baking powder

$1/2$ tsp. salt

3   Tbs. unsalted butter, softened

1   cup buttermilk

$1/4$ cup sesame seeds

Kosher salt

Place the dry ingredients in a mixer with a dough hook. Blend together and dot in softened butter, add buttermilk and sesame seeds, and mix just until dough comes together. Let rest covered in refrigerator.

Divide the dough into 8 equal balls. Roll out with lots of flour into approximately a 10-inch circle. Brush off excess flour. Sprinkle with a small amount of salt and roll in gently.

Bake on a parchment-lined sheet pan at 375°F for approximately 12 minutes until slightly brown. Cool and store in an air-tight container (this recipe makes extra).

APPLE-ONION MARMALADE

3   onions, peeled and thinly sliced

2   Tbs. olive oil

1   Granny Smith apple, peeled and grated with the large side of a grater

$1/2$ cup white wine

Sauté the onions with the olive oil in a heavy-bottomed pan over medium heat until soft and brown. Add the apples and white wine; continue to cook until the liquid comes out of the apples and cooks down to a marmalade consistency. Remove from heat and set aside.

OVEN-DRIED TOMATOES

16   red Roma tomatoes

Salt and pepper

Cut tomatoes in half lengthwise and remove the stem. Place cut-side up on a sheet tray and season with salt and pepper. Bake in a 200°F oven on a rack for 2 to 3 hours until they shrink to $1/2$ their original size. Remove from oven. Let cool and cut each $1/2$ tomato into 3 pieces.

HERB GOAT CHEESE

1   cup soft goat cheese (for lower fat, use low fat ricotta)

1   Tbs. fresh rosemary, chopped

1   Tbs. fresh thyme, chopped

8   garlic cloves, blanched in water for 5 minutes, then puréed

Salt and pepper

Blend all ingredients in a mixer until well incorporated. Season with salt and pepper to taste.

GARNISH

$1/4$ cup Calamata olives, quartered

10   basil leaves, julienned

extra virgin olive oil

To Serve

On each lavosh pizza base, spread $1/4$ cup onion marmalade evenly $1/4$ inch from edge of the crust. Scatter $1/4$ of the tomatoes, olives, and goat cheese on the top. Bake on the top shelf of a 375°F oven for 6 minutes on an upside-down cookie sheet or pizza stone. Remove from oven and sprinkle with basil julienne and drizzle with a small amount of extra virgin olive oil.

PHOTO: *Crispy sesame lavosh pizza with apple-onion marmalade, oven-dried tomatoes, calamata olives, and herb goat cheese*

GRILLED SEA SCALLOPS AND MAINE LOBSTER–SWEET CORN PANCAKE WITH RED PEPPERS, CRISPY BACON, AND WHOLE-GRAIN MUSTARD SAUCE

(Serves 4)

PANCAKE MIX

$^1/_2$ cup heavy cream

$^1/_2$ cup soda water

1 egg yolk

$^1/_4$ cup plus 2 Tbs. corn flour

$^1/_2$ cup all-purpose flour

2 Tbs. stone-ground cornmeal

$^1/_{16}$ tsp. baking powder

$^1/_2$ tsp. sugar

$^3/_4$ cup sautéed spinach, coarsely chopped

$^1/_4$ cup pecan pieces, toasted

$^1/_4$ cup fresh corn kernels, blanched

1 1-lb. lobster, steamed, meat removed from shell and coarsely chopped

6 slices lean bacon, diced and rendered crispy (use $^1/_2$ and reserve $^1/_2$ for garnish)

$^1/_2$ red bell pepper, cut into a very small dice and sautéed in butter

$^1/_4$ cup fresh chives, chopped

Salt, pepper, and cayenne

Blend the flour, cornmeal, baking powder, and sugar in a stainless steel bowl. Set aside. In a blender, add the cream, soda water, and peppers. Pulse 5 to 6 times. Using a whisk, mix the wet into the dry ingredients. Add the egg yolk. Stir in

the spinach, pecans, corn, bacon, lobster, and chives. Season with salt, pepper, and pinch of cayenne.

MUSTARD SAUCE

2	Tbs. shallots, chopped
1/4	cup dry white wine
1	bay leaf
1	thyme sprig
16	oz. chicken or fish stock
12	oz. heavy cream
1	Tbs. whole-grain mustard
1	Tbs. Dijon mustard
	Salt and pepper to taste

Place shallots, wine, bay leaf, thyme, and stock in a sauce pot and reduce until almost dry. Add cream and reduce to sauce consistency. Pass through a fine strainer. Whisk in mustards and season with salt and pepper to taste.

SEA SCALLOPS

8	jumbo sea scallops, cleaned
1	Tbs. Italian parsley, chopped
1	Tbs. olive oil
1	Tbs. thyme, chopped
	Salt and pepper

Toss the scallops with the parsley and oil. Season with salt and pepper. Grill until medium.

GARNISH

1	Tbs. chives, chopped
4	thyme sprigs
1	Roma tomato, seeded and diced small
	Lean bacon, diced and rendered crispy, reserved from before

To Serve

In a heavy-bottomed skillet with a small amount of olive oil, using 1/2 cup of pancake mixture form pancake approximately

3/4-inch thick. Sauté 2 to 3 minutes on each side until lightly brown. Place the pancake in the center of a plate with 2 grilled sea scallops on top. Surround the pancake with the mustard sauce. Sprinkle with chives, tomato, and bacon. Garnish with thyme sprigs.

GRILLED VEGETABLE SANDWICH WITH NEW POTATO SALAD
(Serves 4)

VEGETABLES

1	lg. red bell pepper
1	lg. yellow bell pepper
1–2	med. zucchini
1–2	med. yellow squash
3	portobello mushrooms
1	avocado, sliced into 12 segments
1/4	cup olive oil
2	Tbs. fresh thyme
2	Tbs. fresh chopped rosemary
1	pt. alfalfa sprouts
4	slices of walnut bread (or good quality bread of choice) approximately 1/2" thick, 3" x 5"

Cut the peppers into eighths and remove the seeds. Slice the zucchini and yellow squash into 1/4-inch slices. Remove the stems from the Portobello mushrooms. Place all the vegetables in a bowl and coat well with olive oil and fresh herbs, season with salt and pepper, and reserve.

HUMMUS

1	cup garbanzo beans (chickpeas)
2	Tbs. sesame paste (tahini)
2/3	Tbs. olive oil
1	tsp. garlic puree
2	Tbs. fresh lemon juice
	Salt and pepper to taste

Place all the ingredients in a food processor; blend well. Season with salt and pepper.

SHALLOT-MUSTARD VINAIGRETTE

2 Tbs. Dijon mustard
$^1/_2$ cup champagne vinegar
1 cup extra virgin olive oil
1 cup pure olive oil
$^1/_4$ cup shallots, finely chopped
Salt and pepper to taste

In a stainless steel bowl, mix the mustard in the vinegar. With a wire whisk, add the olive oils in a steady stream until well blended. Add the shallots and season with salt and pepper. This recipe will make extra; reserve in an olive oil bottle and place in the refrigerator.

POTATO SALAD

2 lbs. new potatoes, reds and Yukon golds
2 hard-cooked eggs, chopped coarsely
3 Tbs. Italian parsley, chopped
1 cup shallot-mustard vinaigrette
$^1/_4$ cup red onion, chopped fine

Boil the potatoes in salted water until just tender. Remove and let cool. Cut potatoes into quarters. Mix all of the ingredients together. Let stand for at least 2 hours to allow flavors to blend.

To Serve

Grill vegetables on both sides until lightly brown and tender. Cut the Portobellos into thirds. Lightly brush 4 slices of walnut bread with olive oil and grill 4 to 5 minutes on each side until brown or just until tender yet not too soft. Keep warm. Spread a layer of hummus on the grilled bread. Alternate layers of zucchini, yellow squash, mushrooms, and peppers. Lay slices of avocado on top. Mix the vinaigrette   and drizzle 3 to 4 tablespoons on each sandwich. Garnish with alfalfa sprouts and potato salad.

MARINATED, MUSTARD-GLAZED YELLOWFIN TUNA WITH RED ONION-CUCUMBER SALAD AND AGED BALSAMIC VINAIGRETTE

(Serves 4)

TUNA

4 7-oz. tuna fillets (1 inch thin)
4 oz. olive oil
$^1/_4$ cup soy sauce
4 garlic cloves, crushed
1 orange, juiced and zest grated
1 lemon, juiced and zest grated

Combine the oil, soy, garlic, and citrus juices. Place the tuna in a baking dish and cover with the marinade, making sure all sides are covered.

SALAD

4 cucumbers, peeled, cut in half lengthwise, seeds removed, sliced $^1/_8$-inch thick
1 red onion, peeled, cut in half, sliced paper thin
1 cup seasoned rice wine vinegar
1 tsp. garlic purée
2 tsp. sesame oil
1 tsp. honey
1 tsp. ginger, chopped
1 Tbs. soy sauce
Salt
Pinch cayenne pepper
Pinch chili flakes

Salt the cucumbers and let stand in a strainer for 1 hour. Mix all the ingredients together. Add the cucumbers and onions. Set aside to marinate for 1 hour.

MUSTARD GLAZE

$^1/_4$ cup whole grain mustard
2 Tbs. soy sauce
2 Tbs. red wine vinegar
1 tsp. honey

Mix all ingredients together.

BALSAMIC VINAIGRETTE

$^1/_4$ cup balsamic vinegar

2   Tbs. Dijon mustard

$^1/_2$ cup olive oil

$^1/_2$ cup extra virgin olive oil

    Salt and pepper

In a stainless steel bowl, mix the mustard and vinegar. With a whisk, add the oils in a steady stream until well blended. Season with salt and pepper.

WINE

The Health Benefits of Wine

Recent studies in America, Europe, and Australia indicate that there are significant health benefits from moderate consumption of wine. It started a few years ago with the first study, which became known as the "French Paradox." The French love to eat very rich foods, but they have a glass of wine each day. The study found that the incidence of heart disease in France was lower than in America despite the supposedly poor nutrition habits of the French. Scientists began to investigate and found that having a glass of wine a day with a meal actually had a balancing effect for very rich diets. Initially red wines were believed to be more beneficial than whites, but recent studies show very little difference. Scientific evidence shows that both red and white wine have health benefits when consumed in moderation.

To Serve

Season tuna with salt and pepper. In a heavy-bottomed pan, sear tuna 1 to 2 minutes on each side. Keep it medium rare. Place tuna in the center of a plate. Arrange some cucumber salad on top. Drizzle the balsamic vinaigrette around.

PEAR-LEMON CRÈME BRÛLÉE

(Serves 4)

9   egg yolks

$^3/_4$ cup sugar

2   cups heavy cream

2   cups half and half

$^1/_2$ vanilla bean

$^1/_4$ cup pear William liquor

2   lemons' zest, grated

Bring cream, vanilla bean, and half and half to a boil. Whisk the egg yolk and sugar in a stainless steel bowl until well blended and lemony in color.

Add the hot cream slowly to the egg yolk mixture, whisking constantly. Pass through a fine strainer. Refrigerate overnight.

Add the liquor and lemon zest to the mixture. Ladle into 6-ounce oven-proof ramekins and place in a shallow roasting pan. Fill roasting pan with hot water until it reaches $^1/_4$ from the top of the molds. Bake in a preheated 350°F oven for 50 to 60 minutes until custard is set. Let cool at room temperature and place in the refrigerator until cold.

To Serve

Cover the top with a fine layer of granulated sugar and caramelize with a propane torch or under a very hot broiler. Serve with your favorite biscotti.

STYLE

From the Turquoise Coast

Between the Pillars of Hercules and the Rock of Gibraltar lies the Mediterranean with its ancient civilizations. A Mediterranean-inspired setting creates a beautiful forum for foods and spices from this region.

- Select flatware and dinnerware with details and patterns reminiscent of the area.
- Add flowers in an exotic copper vase.
- Choose glasses with a rough-hewn, pebbled finish.
- Give traditional napkins a special flair with hammered scroll rings.
- Serve Mediterranean-style condiments and breads.
- Add to the ambience of this dinner from the Turquoise Coast with light from candles and lamps.

★ AARON HURDLE

VILLA CHRISTINA
ATLANTA, GEORGIA

APPETIZER

GIANT FRIED CORNMEAL
OYSTERS, ARTICHOKE AIOLI,
FENNEL SALAD GARNI

ENTRÉES

ANGEL HAIR ALLA TUSCAN

FILET MIGNON PARPADELLA

PEPPERED GRILLED RED
SNAPPER AND RISOTTO

DESSERT

TIRAMISU

Executive Chef Aaron Hurdle of Villa Christina in Atlanta, Georgia, first became interested in food and cooking while watching his mother and grandmother working in their kitchen. He began his career in the culinary field as a dishwasher at the Shillington Diner in his hometown of Reading, Pennsylvania. Hurdle's next training came as a Quartermaster for the United States Army, where he spent his entire tour of duty as a chef at the United States Military Academy Prep School in Fort Monmouth, New Jersey.

After finishing his military tour, Chef Hurdle returned to Pennsylvania for the summer to work in the kitchen of the Inn at Reading where he met friends and mentors Allen Rutter, Leo Gonzalez, and Darrell Sweigert. In 1990, Chef Hurdle graduated from Johnson and Wales University in Providence, Rhode Island, and returned to Reading to work as Restaurant Chef for the Inn at Reading and then as Sous Chef for the Butler's Pantry catering service.

In 1994, he accepted the invitation to work as Executive Sous Chef on the opening staff of Villa Christina, a restaurant born from a fairy tale of a downed World War II B-17 pilot and the ravishing Italian countess who nursed him back to health. In fact, the restaurant has the appearance of an Italian villa. It is located on eight acres of manicured lawns, stone bridges, nature paths, and soothing streams. In October of 1995, Chef Hurdle was promoted to the Executive Chef position at Villa Christina. Under Chef Hurdle's direction, Villa Christina was named on *Esquire*'s list of "Best New Restaurants in America" in 1995.

PHOTO: *Tiramisu*

AARON HURDLE

GIANT FRIED CORNMEAL OYSTERS, ARTICHOKE AIOLI, FENNEL SALAD GARNI

(Serves 6 to 8)

OYSTERS

As many as desired

CORNMEAL COATING

- $2/3$ cup cornmeal
- $1/3$ cup flour
- 1   Tbs. garlic powder
- 1   Tbs. onion powder

Salt and white pepper to taste

Mix cornmeal, flour, garlic, and onion powders together and season with salt and pepper. Dredge oysters in seasoned cornmeal and fry until brown. Remove from oil and reserve on a paper towel to absorb the extra oil.

FENNEL SALAD

- 2   lg. fresh fennel bulbs
- $1/2$ cup extra virgin olive oil
- $1/2$ cup white balsamic vinegar
- $1/2$ oz. basil, chopped
- $1/3$ oz. thyme, chopped
- $1/3$ oz. parsley, chopped
- $1/3$ oz. oregano, chopped
- $1/2$ tsp. shallots, minced
- $1/2$ tsp. garlic, minced
- 1   Tbs. lemon juice

Salt and pepper to taste

Remove the stalks from the fennel and cut bulb in half. Remove the root. Take fennel halves and shave fine on a meat slicer to paper thin strips. Combine chopped herbs, shallots, and garlic with oils. Toss fennel with oils, herbs, and lemon juice to coat. Season with salt and pepper.

ARTICHOKE AIOLI

- 1   qt. mayonnaise
- $1/2$ lb. artichoke hearts, salt-water packed, finely chopped
- $1/2$ oz. basil, chopped
- $1/2$ oz. oregano, chopped
- $1/2$ oz. parsley, chopped
- $1/2$ oz. thyme, chopped
- 1   tsp. garlic, minced

Whisk all ingredients to a smooth consistency. Set aside.

PORTOBELLO MUSHROOM BISQUE

- 5   lbs. portobello mushrooms
- 2   Tbs. olive oil
- $1/2$ qt. heavy cream
- $1/2$ qt. chicken stock
- 2   Tbs. chervil, chopped
- 2   Tbs. opal basil

Salt and pepper to taste

Finely chop the mushrooms. In a large sauce pot, sweat mushrooms and olive oil. Add chicken stock and boil for 10 minutes. Add heavy cream, herbs, and seasoning and bring to a second boil. Continue to cook until the soup reaches proper consistency. Strain and keep warm for service.

To Serve

Spoon artichoke aioli into a bowl and place in the center of a serving platter. Place cornmeal oysters around the aioli. Garnish with fennel salad and serve with portobello mushroom bisque.

ANGEL HAIR ALLA TUSCAN

(Serves 6)

- 6   oz. spinach angel hair pasta
- 6   oz. egg angel hair pasta
- 1   cup zucchini, julienned
- 1   cup yellow squash, julienned
- 1   cup carrots, julienned
- $1/2$ cup asparagus, chopped

PHOTO: *Filet mignon parpadella*

1 Tbs. capers
1 oz. Calamata olives
1/2 oz. sun-dried tomatoes
2 tsp. opal basil, finely chopped
4 oz. extra virgin olive oil
4 oz. white balsamic vinegar
2 tsp. fresh garlic, chopped

In boiling salted water, cook the spinach and egg angel hair pasta until al dente. Remove from the water and strain. Saute with fresh vegetables, capers, olives, sun-dried tomatoes, opal basil, extra virgin olive oil, white balsamic vinegar, and chopped garlic.

To Serve

Place pasta in the center of a plate and garnish with opal basil. Serve immediately.

FILET MIGNON PARPADELLA
(Serves 4)

FILET MIGNON

4 7-oz. beef tenderloins, sliced thin
2 Tbs. pink peppercorns
4 Tbs. dark balsamic vinegar
10 oz. demi-glace
20 oz. mesclun mixed greens

Heat olive oil in a sauté pan. Place tenderloin slices in pan. Sauté with 1 teaspoon of pink peppercorns until tenderloin is medium rare. Add 1 ounce of balsamic vinegar and 5 ounces of demi-glace. Salt and pepper to taste. Continue to sauté until balsamic vinegar and demi-glace have blended. Remove from heat.

PARPADELLE CASSEROLE

1	yellow onion, julienned
2	lbs. Parpadelle pasta, cooked
$1/2$	tsp. garlic, finely chopped
1	med. green pepper, finely diced
1	med. red pepper, finely diced
1	med. yellow pepper, finely diced
1	med. zucchini, julienned
1	med. yellow squash, julienned
2	cups Reggiano cheese
1	qt. heavy cream
2	Tbs. parsley, chopped
8	whole eggs
	Salt and white pepper to taste

Sauté the julienne of onion in olive oil until translucent; remove from heat and reserve. Combine cooked parpadelle, garlic, onions, and vegetables in a mixing bowl. Pour inside a 3-inch deep casserole dish making sure to spread evenly.

Whisk eggs and heavy cream in a separate bowl. Add Reggiano cheese, parsley, and salt and pepper to taste. (Make sure to smooth out cheese.) Pour over pasta until the liquid is $1/4$ inch over pasta topping to make sure liquid settles thoroughly. Cover tightly with aluminum foil. Bake at 350°F for $1^1/2$ hours. Check doneness with fork. You may have to continue to cook depending on your oven. Cool on rack overnight.

To Serve

Toss 5 ounces of field greens in mixing bowl with 2 ounces of balsamic vinaigrette. Place on center of dinner plate. Using a $2^1/2$-inch round cookie cutter, cut out a circle of the casserole. Place Parpadelle casserole round on the center of the plate atop greens. Pinwheel tenderloin around the casserole.

Wine Recommendation:
Wente Vineyards Merlot

PEPPERED GRILLED RED SNAPPER AND RISOTTO
(Serves 6)

RISOTTO

3	cups Arborio rice
2	Tbs. garlic, chopped
4	Tbs. olive oil
10	cups chicken stock, warm
4	Tbs. sweet butter
2	bay leaves
1	Tbs. thyme
$1/2$	med. yellow onion, diced
	Salt and fresh cracked pepper
	Parmigiana cheese

Sauté Arborio rice and garlic in olive oil. When hot, add heated chicken stock. Continue to stir until liquid is absorbed. When tender, add butter, bay leaves, thyme, and diced onion and season to taste. Fold in cheese and transfer to sheet pan. Hold for service.

PEPPERED GRILLED RED SNAPPER

6	8-oz. red snapper fillets, skin removed
1	cup olive oil
1	cup fresh cracked pepper
8	oz. kosher salt
16	oz. vegetable stock
10	oz. risotto
2	tsp. unsalted butter
2	Tbs. Asiago cheese

2   oz. tomato concasse

2   oz. leeks, julienned

Salt and white pepper to taste

Remove the skin of an 8-ounce red snapper fillet. Cut fillet
on the bias into 5 pieces. Dip pieces in olive oil and coat with
fresh cracked pepper. Sprinkle with a pinch of kosher salt.
Grill on both sides until cooked through.

In a heavy-bottomed sauté pan over high heat, bring 8
ounces of vegetable stock to a boil. Add 5 ounces of risotto
and cook until stock is absorbed. Add unsalted butter, Asiago
cheese, salt, and white pepper to taste. Add tomato concasse
and sautéed julienned leeks. Simmer all ingredients together.
Stir until smooth and remove from heat after thoroughly
blended.

To Serve

Arrange risotto in the center of a plate. Fan the sautéed
snapper around the risotto and top with sautéed vegetables.
Serve immediately.

TIRAMISU

MASCARPONE CHEESE MIXTURE

3   whole eggs

5   oz. sugar

1   tsp. vanilla extract

5$^1/_2$ oz. mascarpone cheese

10   oz. heavy cream

Beat eggs and sugar in mixer until stiff. Add vanilla and mix.
Add mascarpone cheese and continue to blend until mixture
forms soft peaks. Transfer mixture to a clean bowl and place
in refrigerator to chill. Again using the mixer, beat the heavy
cream until it forms stiff peaks. Fold cream into egg, sugar,
and cheese mixture and return to refrigerator to chill.

LADYFINGERS

$^3/_4$ cup espresso, room temperature

1   Tbs. Amaretto

WINE

The Basics of Pairing Wines with Food

There are some basic guidelines for matching wine with food:

• Serve white wines with white meat such as chicken, poultry, pork, veal, and white-fleshed fish

• Serve red wines with red meats such as beef, lamb, and venison

• Serve aged wines with aged meats

• Serve pink wines or rosés with salads

• Serve sparkling wines with an appetizer and throughout the meal to dessert

• A dessert wine should be at least as sweet as the dessert or it will tend to taste sour.

You can use these simple guidelines, or enjoy breaking the rules and have a light red wine with fish, especially a red-fleshed fish, or a robust white such as a Chardonnay with a steak. Or try a good Cabernet Sauvignon with the filet mignon Parpadelle and a sparkling wine with the tiramisu.

1   Tbs. Kahlua

12   ladyfinger cookies

4   2¹/₂" diameter PVC tubes, 3" in length
     (may be purchased at a hardware supply store)

2   oz. semisweet chocolate for grating

In a bowl combine espresso, Amaretto, and Kahlua and set aside. Cut ladyfingers into 2¹/₂-inch diameter rounds using a cookie cutter. Lightly brush the tops of the ladyfingers with mixture (be careful not to overdo) and set aside.

Place a ladyfinger round in the bottom of a PVC tube. Next, add a layer of the cheese mixture and top with grated chocolate. Add another ladyfinger round, more cheese mixture, and more grated chocolate. Add one more ladyfinger round and place the tube in the freezer to chill for 24 hours.

COFFEE ROCKS

¹/₄ cup espresso, room temperature

¹/₂ cup sugar

In a small bowl, mix espresso and sugar together until crumbs form. Reserve for garnish.

CHOCOLATE CAGE

8   oz. semisweet chocolate

4   5 x 8¹/₂" sheets of 5 mm. plastic sheeting (may
     be purchased at an art supply store)

4   rubber bands

The plastic sheet, once covered with the chocolate design, will be wrapped around the tiramisu to make a delicious cage and decoration. Cut the plastic sheets to 5 inches high by 8¹/₂ inches wide. Starting at one end, measure up 3 inches high and make a 2-inch long cut toward the center of the plastic. Repeat this process on the other side. With the remaining plastic at the top of the sheet cut a half circle. Repeat this process for all 4 sheets. Other designs may be substituted. Melt the chocolate in a double boiler. Once the chocolate is completely melted, transfer it to a pastry bag,

and using a narrow tip begin making small circles on the plastic, make sure all the circles' edges touch. Repeat this process for all of the sheets, reheating the chocolate in hot water when necessary. Set the plastic sheets aside to cool.

FUDGE SAUCE (OPTIONAL OR IN PLACE OF CHOCOLATE CAGE)

¹/₂ cup sweet dark chocolate

6   oz. heavy cream

1   tsp. vanilla extract

Melt chocolate in a stainless steel bowl over boiling water. In another stainless steel bowl, bring heavy cream to a boil. Reduce heat to a simmer and add vanilla extract; if the temperature is too hot, the cream and chocolate will separate. Pour cream into the melted chocolate and stir continuously until well mixed. Remove from heat and allow to cool.

ESPRESSO WHIPPED CREAM

1   cup heavy whipping cream

1   Tbs. espresso, room temperature

2   Tbs. sugar

In a chilled bowl, add the heavy cream and sugar and beat to stiff peaks. Fold in the espresso and chill until ready for garnish.

To Serve

Remove the PVC tubes from the freezer. Carefully push the tiramisu out of the tube and place in the center of a plate. Turn the oven on to low and place the chocolate design in the oven for just a second to warm the chocolate. Wrap the plastic around the tiramisu and place a rubber band around it to hold it in place. Chill the tiramisu in the refrigerator for 15 minutes. Remove the plastic, garnish with a generous spoonful of espresso whipped cream and sprinkle with coffee rocks.

STYLE

A Family Affair

Many of our important moments are spent with our families. Welcoming new people into our lives together can be a lovely and gracious tradition.

For your family affair, a plain white tablecloth chronicles those who have broken bread there. As a new relative or friend is welcomed, they write their name in pencil somewhere on the cloth. Later, embroider the signature with brightly colored thread to save the moment for years.

Gold band dinnerware, white cotton napkins, and elegant braided brass napkin rings are flawless and simple.

A flower at each place setting adds color and candles remind guests that they are welcome at your table.

Around the room are the treasures capturing the moments that have made your lives so full.

MICHAEL OTSUKA

PATINA

LOS ANGELES, CALIFORNIA

APPETIZER

PAPPA AL POMODORO OR
TOMATO BREAD SOUP

ENTRÉES

ROASTED EGGPLANT CANNEL-
LONI WITH A TRUFFLE-SCENTED
TOMATO SAUCE AND SOFT
HERBS

COQ AU VIN WITH A TRIO OF
CARAMELIZED ROOT VEGETA-
BLES AND THEIR CHIPS

GRILLED PAILLARD OF SWORD-
FISH WITH ARGENTINEAN-STYLE
VEGETABLE COMPOTE

DESSERT

CARAMELIZED MANGO-LIME
TART WITH PISTACHIO CRUST
AND TOASTED COCONUT CREAM

Executive Chef Michael Otsuka of Patina in Los Angeles, California first became interested in the culinary arts by cooking alongside his mother and grandmother. He recalls spending hours in his childhood stirring, stewing, and baking the traditional foods of his diverse ethnic heritage. Chef Otsuka's mother was Jewish-Viennese and his paternal grandparents were Japanese emigrants.

In 1983, Chef Otsuka began his culinary training. He apprenticed to Joachim Splichal at his Seventh Street Bistro in Los Angeles. Splichal brought Otsuka to his next restaurant, the acclaimed Max au Triangle in Beverly Hills. Less than two years later Otsuka was named Sous Chef.

After working as a personal chef to an affluent Michigan family, Michael continued his training in Europe, where he worked in the kitchens of two one-star Michelin restaurants: Kasteel St. Paul at Lumen, Belgium, and Hotel Restaurant Leonce in Florençac. Chef Otsuka apprenticed in two two-star Michelin restaurants: with Jacques Maximin at the Hotel Negresco in Nice and the restaurant Michel Bras in Laguiole. In 1992, Chef Otsuka returned to Los Angeles and to his mentor Splichal to work in the kitchen of Patina as Sous Chef, and then on to open Pinot Bistro where he spent three years and was a driving force as the Chef de Cuisine. In July of 1995, Chef Otsuka was promoted to Executive Chef of Patina. In 1996, he was honored as a nominee for Rising Star Chef by the James Beard Foundation.

PHOTO: *Grilled paillard of swordfish with Argentinean-style vegetable compote*

MICHAEL OTSUKA

PAPPA AL POMODORO OR TOMATO BREAD SOUP
(Serves 4)

3 lbs. ripe Roma tomatoes, tops cut off and discarded, chopped

6 cloves garlic, peeled and sliced

$1/2$ cup olive oil

3 lg. leeks, washed well, white part only, roughly chopped

1 lg. onion, peeled and large diced

1 lg. carrot, peeled and large diced

2 lg. celery stalks, washed and coarse cut

$1/2$ cup white wine

3 bay leaves

3 branches fresh thyme

1 bunch fresh basil, leaves picked and sliced fine, reserve stems

1 sm. piece cheese cloth

12 inches kitchen string

$1^1/2$ qt. chicken stock

3 cups bread, cut into small croutons and dried in the oven

1 cup Parmesan cheese

1 Tbs. coriander seed

4 Tbs. black pepper

Kosher salt and freshly ground white pepper to taste

In a heavy-bottomed stock pot, place the olive oil and all the vegetables except tomatoes over a medium flame. Do not allow the vegetables to color. Cook slowly until they are wilted and translucent. Put the thyme, basil stems, and bay leaves in cheese cloth and tie firmly. Place the bag in the pot with the tomatoes and white wine. Cook slowly until the raw wine flavor is cooked out. Add chicken stock and simmer for 15 minutes. Remove cloth bag, pressing it between spoons in order to extract the maximum flavor, and discard. Carefully purée soup in small batches to a coarse texture. Return to the pot and season to taste with kosher salt and freshly ground white pepper. The soup may be prepared to this point up to two days in advance.

Toss the dried bread croutons with sliced basil leaves, a little olive oil, and plenty of Parmesan cheese.

To Serve

Heat the soup until very hot and pour into heated soup bowls over basil and Parmesan cheese coated croutons. The finished soup should have a very thick porridge look. Garnish the bowls with a few small leaves of basil, a drizzle of olive oil, and some shaved cheese.

ROASTED EGGPLANT CANNELLONI WITH A TRUFFLE-SCENTED TOMATO SAUCE AND SOFT HERBS
(Serves 4)

EGGPLANT STUFFING

8 med. Japanese eggplants

1 garlic head

4 Tbs. olive oil

1 red onion

6 sun-dried tomatoes (oil-packed type), drained and finely chopped

1 tsp. fennel seed

1 tsp. coriander seed

$1/2$ bunch Italian parsley, washed, sprigs picked and chopped

2 Tbs. fresh thyme, chopped

$1/4$ cup Italian parsley, chopped

Kosher salt and freshly ground white pepper to taste

Roll eggplant in extra virgin olive oil, season with kosher salt and freshly ground white pepper, and roast at 375°F for 30 minutes or until they are fork tender. Allow to cool. Chop roasted eggplant into a coarse purée. Place in a large bowl and set aside. Peel the garlic head and roast until tender in a foil pouch with 2 tablespoons of olive oil. Peel the onion and finely dice. Sauté in olive oil until caramelized and remove from

PHOTO: *Pappa al pomodoro or tomato bread soup*

To cook egg roll wraps, drop into a shallow pot of boiling salted water a few at a time, making sure that they are separate. Cook wraps until al dente (take out of water while there is a hint of firmness to the touch). Pull them out with a slotted wire skimmer and place immediately into a bowl of ice water. On a clean work surface, lay out 6 to 8 wraps flat and spoon eggplant filling onto the lower third of each wrap, about $^1/_3$ cup per wrap, and roll gently into a cylinder. Transfer cannellonis seam side down to a cookie sheet lined with foil that has been lightly brushed with extra virgin olive oil. Brush the tops of the cannellonis with oil and place in a preheated 325°F oven for 15 minutes before serving.

TOMATO COULIS

12 ripe Roma tomatoes
2 oz. white truffle-infused oil
(available in specialty stores)
Kosher salt and freshly ground
White pepper to taste

Blanch the tomatoes; peel, cut in 2 horizontally, and seed. Purée in a food processor or blender and place in a large wire strainer lined with a single layer of damp cheesecloth. Allow coulis to sit over a vessel that is deep enough to allow the water in the tomatoes to pass through. Drain in a cool place for at least 2 hours. "Tomato water" may be reserved for another usage. Heat $1^1/_2$ cups of the tomato coulis and season to taste. Whisk in the oil at the last second before serving.

heat. Toast the fennel and coriander seeds separately, remove from pan, and process in a spice mill or coffee mill. Fold in the remaining ingredients. Season with Kosher salt and freshly ground white pepper to taste.

PASTA

1   package Chinese egg roll wraps

SOFT HERB SALAD

$1^1/_2$ cups mixed soft herbs

4 Tbs. shallots, chopped

3 Tbs. balsamic vinegar

5 Tbs. extra virgin olive oil

Use any combination that does not include the harder flavors or textures such as rosemary, thyme, marjoram, et cetera. A combination that works well, depending on availability, is small basil leaves, Italian parsley sprigs, young tarragon leaves, Daikon radish sprouts, lentil sprouts, chives cut into 1-inch lengths, golden leaves from the celery heart, baby mizunna, baby spinach, baby arugula, Opal basil leaves, leaves and flowers from the nasturtium plant, and borrage blossoms. The mix should have a lot of contrast. Add shallots to herb mix and season to taste. Add the vinegar and olive oil just to lightly coat the salad.

To Serve

In four warm large pasta bowls, place the cannellonis carefully side by side. Spoon over the tomato coulis and garnish the pasta with a mound of herb salad gently placed at the center of each plate. Garnish with freshly shaved Parmesan if desired.

COQ AU VIN WITH A TRIO OF CARAMELIZED ROOT VEGETABLES AND THEIR CHIPS

(Serves 4 with leftovers)

CHICKEN MARINADE

2 $4^1/_2$- lb. chickens cut into 8 pieces each (breasts cut in 2, leaving the first joint of the wing intact; thigh and drumstick separated; reserve backs for other use

2 Tbs. cracked black pepper

Cabernet style red wine (enough to cover)

Season the chicken pieces with the pepper and place in a container that can hold them comfortably. Cover with the Cabernet and allow to marinate at least 4 days, but best if allowed to marinate for 6 to 7.

2 cups onion, finely diced

1 cup celery, finely diced

2 cups white mushrooms, thinly sliced

$1/_4$ cup garlic, minced

1 bouquet garni: (wrap in cheese cloth and secure with kitchen string 4 bay leaves, 3 cloves, $1/_4$ bunch of thyme sprigs, stems from 1 bunch of parsley, $1/_4$ bunch of fresh savory sprigs)

4 oz. apple-smoked bacon, diced

All-purpose flour

RESERVED MARINADE

$3/_4$ cup peanut oil

Kosher salt to taste

Drain chicken parts. Pat dry with paper towels and season. Roll in flour and shake off excess. Heat enough peanut oil to liberally cover the bottom of a large, heavy sauté pan until it begins to smoke. Carefully brown the pieces on all sides and place in a pot that will accommodate all the chicken. Clean sauté pan and use to sauté the bacon until crispy. Add bacon to the pot and use the drippings to sauté the onions, garlic, mushrooms, and celery until lightly colored and tender. Place vegetables and bouquet garni in with the chicken and cover with the reserved marinade, adding more wine if necessary to cover.

Bring to a slow simmer and braise for about 40 minutes or until chicken is tender. Discard bouquet garni and remove chicken from the braising liquid. Raise flame and allow the liquid to reduce to a sauce-like consistency. Adjust seasoning in sauce. Return chicken to the sauce and keep hot until serving.

VEGETABLES

8 lg. carrots, peeled (reserve stems for chips)

10 lg. parsnips, peeled (reserve stems for chips)

3 yams, peeled

$1/4$ cup butter, cut into small pieces

$1/4$ cup peanut oil

Salt and cracked black pepper to taste

Cut all but 2 parsnips and 2 carrots on the bias about $1/4$-inch thick. Cut 2 of the yams into quarters lengthwise and slice into $1/4$-inch wedges. Heat peanut oil in a large, heavy sauté pan and add the butter. When the butter begins to brown, add the yams and carrots and stir constantly until they begin to caramelize. Add the parsnips and continue to stir until the vegetables are tender and have a light caramel color. Season to taste with salt and cracked black pepper.

VEGETABLE CHIPS

Carrot stems

Parsnip stems

$1/4$ cup Italian parsley, chopped

$1/4$ cup corn starch

$1/2$ cup all-purpose flour

Peanut oil for deep-frying

Salt and freshly ground white pepper to taste

In a deep fryer or heavy deep sauce pot, heat peanut oil to 350°F. Using a vegetable peeler, create thin ribbons of the left-over roots. Keep them separate. Sift together the flour and corn starch and dust the ribbons. Fry in small batches until crisp and golden colored. Season lightly with salt and freshly ground white pepper and sprinkle with the chopped parsley. Mix the chips together. Store in a dry place.

To Serve

On a large serving platter with a raised rim, mound the hot root vegetables in the center and arrange the chicken pieces around them. Ladle a little sauce over the chicken only. Garnish the platter with the crispy chips and whole Italian parsley sprigs. Serve additional sauce on the side.

GRILLED PAILLARD OF SWORDFISH WITH ARGENTINEAN-STYLE VEGETABLE COMPOTE

(Serves 4)

SWORDFISH

4 6-oz. swordfish filets, cut $1/4$-inch thick

1 lemon, juiced

$1/4$ cup extra virgin olive oil

6 garlic cloves, roasted till tender

Marinate swordfish with lemon juice and $1/4$ cup of olive oil. Start a charcoal grill or gas grill to high heat.

ARGENTINEAN-STYLE VEGETABLE COMPOTE

$1/4$ cup red wine vinegar

$3/4$ cup extra virgin olive oil

2 red bell peppers, cut into $1/2$-inch dice

2 yellow bell peppers, cut into $1/2$-inch dice

1 lg. red onion, cut into $1/2$-inch dice

1 fennel bulb, cut into $1/2$-inch dice

1 med. zucchini squash

1 med. Japanese eggplant

$1/2$ bunch Italian parsley, sprigs picked and coarse chopped

$1/2$ bunch oregano, sprigs picked and coarse chopped

1 tsp. cracked black pepper

Kosher salt to taste

Place red and yellow bell peppers on the charcoal or gas grill. Turn occasionally, allowing skin to char on all sides. Once the skin is evenly charred, remove from the grill and immediately place in an ice bath to stop the cooking process. After the peppers have cooled, hold under running water to peel away the charred skin. Seed the peppers and cut into a $1/2$-inch dice. Dice the onion and fennel, toss with olive oil and pan roast until tender and caramelized. Remove from heat to cool. Cut the zucchini squash and eggplant into $1/2$-inch strips and grill until tender; remove from heat, chill, and cut into cubes. Toss all of the vegetables and herbs together and add the vinegar. Season to taste and add the olive oil. This compote will keep, and even get better, covered tightly in the refrigerator for a day.

GARNISH

1   bunch watercress, leaves only

To Serve

Grill swordfish to a medium temperature, approximately 2 minutes on each side, and place on large dinner plates. Garnish with the compote and some watercress leaves. If desired, roasted potatoes would accompany this dish very well.

WINE

Pairing Wine with Fish

A dry, light white wine goes well with light-fleshed fish. Look for a Sauvignon Blanc or a lighter-style Chardonnay that will match the weight of the fish; the weight of the wine and how it feels in your mouth should be the same as the weight of the food itself. So, a light fish goes with a lighter wine and a heavier fish requires a more robust wine, perhaps even a red such as a Gamay Beaujolais or Pinot Noir.

With swordfish, which is firmer and meatier, you want a heavier wine. If you stay with the traditional white, select a full-bodied Chardonnay; the full body will go with the denser swordfish. Grilling the swordfish will give it a smoky character which can be matched with a barrel-aged Chardonnay or a Gamay Beaujolais.

CARAMELIZED MANGO-LIME TART WITH A PISTACHIO CRUST AND TOASTED COCONUT CREAM

(Serves 6)

LIME CUSTARD

6   egg yolks

1   cup sugar

$^1/_2$ cup lime juice and the zest from 2 limes, chopped fine

$^1/_2$ cup butter, cut into small cubes

2   packages gelatin

In a bowl, whisk together the yolks, sugar, and lime juice and zest, then pour into a nonreactive sauce pot with the butter. Bring to a slow simmer, stirring often, until the custard simmers at a slow boil for at least 1 minute. Soften the gelatin in 3 tablespoons of water and set aside. Pour the custard through a wire mesh strainer into a clean bowl, stir in gelatin until well mixed, and refrigerate. This step may be done several days in advance.

MANGOES

2   large mangoes, firm but ripe with a strong aroma

$^1/_2$ cup confectioners' sugar

1   propane torch for caramelizing

With a sharp paring knife, peel the mangoes and split horizontally as close to the stone as possible. Slice long, even strips into each of the 4 halves, carefully avoiding cutting all the way through to the end. One side of the mango should remain intact so as to create a fan look when arranged on the tarts. Transfer with a spatula to a buttered, foil-lined sheet pan. Using a small metal strainer, sift powdered sugar over the mangoes. Warm in the oven slightly before assembling.

PISTACHIO CRUST TART SHELL

1   pkg. phyllo dough, defrosted

$^3/_4$ cup pistachios, unsalted out of the shell, lightly toasted, and coarsely ground

4   oz. sweet unsalted butter, melted

$^1/_4$ cup raw granulated sugar

On a cutting board, lay down a piece of foil the size of a sheet of phyllo dough. Cover foil with a leaf of pastry and, using a pastry brush, coat with a thin layer of butter. Sprinkle a layer of pistachios and raw sugar over. Repeat the process until you have 6 layers of phyllo. Transfer by pulling the foil gently onto a cookie sheet and refrigerate. Once cold, cut into 4 5" x 5" squares and bake in a preheated oven at 350°F until they become an even light blond.

COCONUT CREAM

$^1/_2$ cup coconut, grated, unsweetened, toasted on a cookie sheet until light blond in color

$^1/_2$ cup heavy cream

Whip cream until soft peaks form, add coconut, and continue to whip until firm but not dry.

To Serve

Spread each tart shell with a generous layer of lime custard and place a mango half on each. Using a propane torch, caramelize the tops of the mangoes, being careful not to get the lime custard too hot. Transfer tarts to serving plates and garnish with the coconut cream and any leftover ground pistachios or toasted coconut.

STYLE

A Literary Luncheon

Do you have friends who love to eat and love to read? If so, throw a literary luncheon and discuss the latest best sellers or Proust.

Create a diningroom setting with table and sideboard arrangements that reflects your commitment to literature.

On the table, start with a floral arrangement, then add place mats in bright colors and luxurious napkins on white plates to lend texture and color to the uncovered table. Use some of your favorite

books as the centerpiece.

Candles make ready your literary luncheon table for your main course of food, fun, and good friends. It is simple, elegant, and reflects a deep passion for food for the body and for the soul.

DAVID REARDON

BROWN'S BEACH HOUSE RESTAURANT,
THE ORCHID AT MAUNA LANI
KOHALA COAST, HAWAII

APPETIZERS

CRISP, TARO-CRUSTED 'OPAKA-PAKA AND GRILLED LEEK-FENNEL COMPOTE ON A ROASTED WAIMEA CORN AND GINGER SAUCE WITH MIREPOIX OF VEGETABLES

HERBED EGGPLANT, POTATO, AND TOMATO TORTE WITH ANCHO CHILE SAUCE

ENTRÉES

HERBED, ROASTED BREAST OF FREE RANGE CHICKEN WITH PUNA GOAT CHEESE, YUKON GOLD POTATOES, ARUGULA, SHERRY, MUSTARD, AND PINK PEPPERCORN VINAIGRETTE

PAN-SEARED PACIFIC SALMON IN A WASABI-GINGER CRUST WITH AMA EBI, LEEK CREAMED POTATOES, AND A MAUI ONION JUS

DESSERT

WARM BANANA-CHOCOLATE BREAD PUDDING WITH CARAMEL SAUCE, KONA COFFEE ICE CREAM, AND BERRIES

"The most rewarding culinary experience is a feast for the senses. The delicate aroma of the freshest local herbs, the visually satisfying presentation, a level of service that is unsurpassed, all come together to form a complete dining experience," exclaims Executive Chef David Reardon of Brown's Beach House Restaurant at The Orchid at Mauna Lani.

In 1977, Chef Reardon received a degree in Business Administration from Massachusetts Bay Community College, and three years later he entered ITT Sheraton's Executive Chef Training Program. He has been dazzling epicureans with his culinary prowess from Boston to Hawaii ever since.

Chef Reardon is a co-founder of ITT Sheraton's "Cuisine of the Americas," a newly released program that focuses on the diversity of foods, seasonings, and styles unique to the cultures and societies of the Western Hemisphere, featuring delicious recipes that are low in fat content and calories.

In his eighteen years in the kitchen, Chef Reardon has competed in nearly twenty American Culinary Foundation Shows and won honors and medals in each. A member of the Texas Culinary Olympic Team since 1985, Chef Reardon won gold, silver, and bronze medals in the prestigious IKA/HOGA Culinary Olympics. Overall, his team placed third among twenty-nine other competitive countries and fourteen regional US teams, capturing ten regional medals.

As General Manager/Executive Chef, Reardon secured a five star award for Laurels at the Sheraton Park Central Hotel in Dallas.

In his new position as Director of Culinary Services at The Orchid at Mauna Lani on the island of Hawaii, Chef Reardon's keen sense of product and creative adaptability will take full advantage of the abundance of resources from Hawaii's land and sea. No doubt he will take the island culinary experience to a new level.

PHOTO: *Herbed, roasted breast of free range chicken with puna goat cheese, yukon gold potatoes, arugula, sherry, mustard, and pink peppercorn vinaigrette*

DAVID REARDON

CRISP TARO-CRUSTED 'OPAKAPAKA AND GRILLED LEEK-FENNEL COMPOTE ON A ROASTED WAIMEA CORN AND GINGER SAUCE WITH MIREPOIX OF VEGETABLES
(Serves 6)

CRISP CRUSTED 'OPAKAPAKA

6   4-oz. 'opakapaka fillet (Hawaiian snapper; substitute any white fish)

3   oz. olive oil

3   taro root peel (tropical Asiatic plant)

2   eggs, slightly beaten

Salt and pepper

Flour for dusting

Clean, rinse, and pat fillets dry. Season with salt and pepper, dust with flour, and dredge in egg wash. Slice taro approximately paper thin, using a round $^5/_8$-inch cutter. Do not rinse taro rounds. Place the taro rounds, starting from tail end moving forward in rows horizontally progressing vertically, resembling fish scales.

Heat a sauté pan until olive oil is hot, then carefully place filet with the taro side down in the pan. Sauté until golden brown; carefully flip filet to finish cooking. Reserve.

GRILLED LEEK-FENNEL COMPOTE

6   leeks, cleaned white part, slit in half

2   fennel bulbs, cleaned and sliced

2   Tbs. olive oil

2   lg. shallots

1   cup white wine

2   bay leaves

4   thyme sprigs

1   qt. heavy cream

2   Tbs. orange marmalade

1   tsp. salt

Fresh ground white pepper

Brush leek and fennel with olive oil and place on hot grill. Char evenly and remove. Let cool and julienne. In a hot sauté pan, add 1 teaspoon olive oil and sauté shallots, leeks, and fennel for 2 to 3 minutes. Add white wine, bay leaves, and thyme sprigs. Reduce wine by $^3/_4$ and add heavy cream. Reduce until mixture becomes thick. Add marmalade, salt, and pepper. Remove bay leaves and thyme sprigs and reserve. Keep warm.

ROASTED WAIMEA CORN AND GINGER SAUCE

4   ears Waimea corn (2 cups of kernels)

2   Tbs. olive oil

1   Mahi red onion, diced

1   tsp. garlic, chopped

1   Hawaiian chili pepper, diced

1   Tbs. ginger, grated

1   qt. rich chicken stock

1   cup heavy cream

1   tsp. cumin

$^1/_2$ tsp. salt

Freshly ground white pepper to taste

Roast corn in husk at 375°F for about 25 to 30 minutes. Remove, let cool, and clean kernels off of the cob. Reserve cobs. In a heavy saucepan, add chicken stock and corn cobs. Simmer for 20 minutes. Discard cobs and hold stock.

In a heavy saucepan, heat the olive oil and Mahi onion and sweat for 2 minutes. Add garlic, chili pepper, and ginger; stir for 1 minute. Add stock and corn kernels. Simmer for 20 minutes, add cream, and blend. Add cumin, salt, and pepper. Strain and reserve for service.

VEGETABLE MIREPOIX

2   Tbs. unsalted butter

30   baton carrots, blanched

30   baton celery, blanched

18   pearl onions, peeled, blanched

1   Tbs. dill, chopped

Salt and freshly ground pepper

In a sauté pan, melt butter and lightly sauté vegetables and dill and season. Serve immediately.

To Serve

Place 3 ounces of leek-fennel compote in the center of a warm plate. Place taro-crusted 'opakapaka on top. Ladle 2 ounces of Waimea corn and ginger sauce and place seasoned mirepoix of vegetables around the outer rim. Serve immediately.

HERBED EGGPLANT, POTATO, AND TOMATO TORTE WITH ANCHO CHILE SAUCE

(Serves 6)

EGGPLANT LAYER

2   eggplants, cut lengthwise, $^3/_4$" thick
$^1/_2$ cup flour
1   tsp. salt
$^1/_2$ tsp. freshly ground black pepper
4   eggs, lightly beaten
1   cup Panko (Japanese bread crumbs)
$^1/_2$ cup Parmesan cheese
$^1/_2$ cup olive oil
$^1/_2$ cup Swiss cheese
Basil sprigs and chopped chives for garnish

Cut eggplant into 12 3-inch-round circles, approximately $^3/_4$-inch thick. Combine flour with salt and pepper, and bread crumbs with Parmesan cheese. Dip eggplant circles in flour mixture, egg, and bread crumbs, patting to evenly coat. In medium saucepan, heat olive oil on moderately high heat. Sauté breaded eggplant slices on both sides until golden brown. Remove and drain on paper towels to cool.

POTATO LAYER

2   baking potatoes
$^1/_2$ cup onions, diced
1   Tbs. unsalted butter
2   tsp. garlic, chopped
$^1/_2$ cup Parmesan cheese
$^1/_2$ cup mozzarella cheese
1   Tbs. basil, chopped
1   Tbs. parsley, chopped
Hawaiian salt
Freshly ground black pepper

Place whole potatoes in a sauce pot of lightly salted cold water and cook at low heat until potatoes are tender (approximately 20 minutes). Drain and cool potatoes. Peel off the skin and grate. In a sauté pan, cook the diced onions in butter until translucent. Add garlic and let cool. Add the onions and garlic to the grated potato with basil, parsley, Parmesan cheese, and mozzarella. Add salt and pepper to taste.

SPINACH LAYER

2   Tbs. unsalted butter
1   lb. fresh spinach, washed and stemmed
Hawaiian salt
Freshly ground black pepper

In a small saucepan, melt the butter, add spinach, and sauté over moderately-high heat until spinach is wilted. Season with salt and pepper and transfer to a strainer. Squeeze off excess liquid. Cool and set aside.

TOMATO LAYER

1   Tbs. olive oil
$^1/_4$ cup shallots, minced
2   tsp. garlic cloves, diced
$^1/_2$ cup tomatoes, blanched, seeded, and diced
2   tsp. fresh oregano, minced
1   Tbs. fresh basil leaves, minced
1   Tbs. capers, diced

In a small saucepan, heat olive oil. Add shallots and stir for a few minutes until softened. Add garlic and tomatoes; sauté for a few minutes. Add fresh oregano and basil. Remove from heat and add diced capers.

ANCHO CHILE SAUCE

4   lg. dried Ancho chilies
1   Tbs. peanut oil

1½ cups onions, minced

1 Tbs. fennel seed

2 Tbs. garlic, minced

2 tsp. serrano chili, minced (optional)

½ cup fresh chicken stock

½ cup dry red wine

1 cup tomato, seeded, diced

½ tsp. cinnamon

⅔ cup heavy cream

2 tsp. macadamia nut honey, or to taste

1 Tbs. fresh lime juice, or to taste

¼ cup cilantro leaves, minced

Salt and freshly ground pepper

Cover chilies in hot water and soak for 30 minutes. Drain and remove stems and seeds. Set aside. Heat oil in a saucepan and sauté onion for 2 to 3 minutes until softened. Add fennel, garlic, and serrano chili and sauté 3 minutes longer. Add stock, wine, tomato, cinnamon, and Ancho chilies and simmer 15 to 20 minutes. Add cream and heat through.

Transfer mixture to a food processor and purée until smooth. Add honey and lime to taste. Strain if desired. Stir in cilantro leaves and adjust seasoning with salt and pepper.

To Serve

Using a lightly-oiled 3-inch-diameter mold, place an eggplant circle at the bottom of the mold and add 3 tablespoons of potato mixture. Press with the back of a spoon, and follow with a layer of the spinach mixture and a layer of tomato mixture. Place Swiss cheese on top. Place the second piece of breaded eggplant on top. Bake at 350°F for 15 minutes or until heated through and the cheese starts to melt. Serve with 2 ounces of ancho chili sauce. Garnish with chilies and basil sprigs.

HERBED, ROASTED BREAST OF FREE RANGE CHICKEN WITH PUNA GOAT CHEESE, YUKON GOLD POTATOES, ARUGULA, SHERRY, MUSTARD, AND PINK PEPPERCORN VINAIGRETTE

(Serves 6)

OVEN-DRIED TOMATOES

6 Roma tomatoes

Cut into quarters and place skin down on a baking sheet in an oven at 200°F for 3 hours. Remove from oven and let cool.

SHERRY, MUSTARD, AND PINK PEPPERCORN VINAIGRETTE

(Makes 2 cups)

2 Tbs. Dijon mustard

1 Tbs. Pommery mustard

3 oz. sherry wine vinegar

10 oz. extra virgin olive oil

1 tsp. Hawaiian salt

½ tsp. freshly ground black pepper

4 Tbs. Italian parsley, chopped

¼ cup pink peppercorns

In a stainless steel bowl, whisk the mustard and sherry wine vinegar together. Drizzle in the olive oil. While whisking, blend in salt, pepper, parsley, and peppercorns. Set aside.

CHICKEN GLAZE

12 oz. chicken stock

In a saucepan, bring chicken stock to a simmer and reduce by ½. Reduce heat and keep warm for garnish.

HERBED, ROASTED BREAST OF FREE-RANGE CHICKEN

6 8–10-oz. chicken breasts from 5-lb. chickens, with rib bones on

10 oz. olive oil

12 basil leaves

1 tsp. Hawaiian salt

1   tsp. freshly ground black pepper

Preheat oven to 375°F. Lift the skin of the chicken and season with salt, black pepper, and 2 basil leaves on each breast. Brush each breast with olive oil, place on a roasting pan, and bake for 15 minutes. Let the chicken rest 5 minutes, remove breast bone, and finish cooking for another 5 minutes. Remove from heat and reserve.

MAUI ONIONS

3   Maui onions, peeled
12 oz. sherry, mustard, and pink peppercorn vinaigrette

Cut onions into sixths and brush with the vinaigrette. Bake for 10 to 12 minutes at 350°F until wilted. Season with salt and pepper and reserve.

YUKON GOLD POTATOES

9   Yukon gold potato, partially cooked (spit)
1   Tbs. fresh rosemary
1   Tbs. olive oil
2   Tbs. garlic cloves, roughly chopped
1   tsp. Hawaiian salt
1   tsp. freshly ground black pepper

In a small bowl, toss the potatoes with rosemary, garlic, salt, and black pepper. Roast in the oven at 375°F for 20 minutes. Reserve for service.

PUNA GOAT CHEESE

1¹/₂ cups Puna goat cheese
1   Tbs. Italian parsley
1   Tbs. fresh oregano
1   Tbs. fresh tarragon
6   slices Parma ham, julienned

Combine in a mixing bowl the softened goat cheese with the Italian parsley, tarragon, oregano, and Parma ham. Blend until smooth and set aside.

PHOTO: *Herbed eggplant, potato and tomato torte with ancho chile sauce*

ARUGULA

3   oz. sherry, mustard, and pink peppercorn viniagrette
6   cups arugula
Salt and pepper

In a medium-sized bowl, toss arugula with the viniagrette. Season with salt and pepper and reserve for service.

To Serve

Place 2 tablespoons of the herbed goat cheese under the skin of the chicken. Heat the chicken in an oven at 350°F for 7 to 8 minutes, making sure the cheese does not run out from under the skin.

Place the arugula in the center of the plate. Slice the chicken breast 4 times and place on top of the arugula. Set the garlic roast potato, onion fans, and oven-dried tomatoes

around the chicken. Drizzle with vinaigrette and chicken glaze.

Wine Recommendation
Bernardus Chardonnay

PAN-SEARED PACIFIC SALMON IN A WASABI-GINGER CRUST WITH AMA EBI, LEEK CREAMED POTATOES, AND A MAUI ONION JUS

(Serves 6)

PACIFIC SALMON

6   6-oz. pieces of Pacific salmon

WASABI-GINGER CRUST

1   Tbs. wasabi paste
1   Tbs. fresh ginger, grated
1   Tbs. orange zest, chopped
3   Tbs. unsalted butter, softened
$^1/_2$ tsp. Hawaiian salt
Fresh cracked black pepper
$^1/_2$ cup Panko (Japanese bread crumbs)

In a small bowl, combine wasabi, ginger, Panko, and orange zest and mix together. Brush each piece of salmon with softened butter and sprinkle with wasabi mixture. Sprinkle with cracked black pepper and salt. Press firmly so that the Panko crust will stick to the top of the salmon filet.

LEEK CREAMED POTATOES

24   oz. Yukon gold potatoes, peeled
1   Tbs. unsalted butter
1   cup leeks, julienned
6   oz. light cream
Salt and freshly ground white pepper

In a heavy sauce pot, boil the potatoes in lightly salted water until very tender. Drain and reserve. In a saucepan, heat 1 tablespoon unsalted butter, add leeks and sweat for a few min-

utes. Add cream, heat, then blend cream mixture into warm potato and mix thoroughly using a stiff whip. Season with salt and pepper and set aside.

AMA EBI

12   ama ebi prawns
$^1/_4$ cup tarragon, chopped
$^1/_4$ cup basil, chopped
$^1/_4$ cup parsley, chopped
2   cups flour
1   tsp. salt
$^1/_4$ tsp. white pepper
6   egg whites, lightly beaten
1   oz. olive oil

Peel and devein prawns. Mix together the fresh herbs. Lightly dust the prawns in flour and season with salt and pepper. Dip in the egg white batter then in herb mixture. Sauté in a pan with olive oil until cooked on both sides. Reserve for service.

MAUI ONION JUS

6   Tbs. sweet butter
$^1/_2$ cup shallots, peeled, sliced
2   cups Maui onions, julienned
2   oz. sherry vinegar
1   qt. rich brown chicken stock
2   tsp. fresh thyme
1   Tbs. chives and Italian parsley, chopped for garnish
Salt and freshly ground white pepper

In a heavy sauce pot, heat 2 tablespoons of butter and sweat the shallots and onions for 3 to 4 minutes. Add vinegar and reduce by $^1/_2$. Add chicken stock and thyme and reduce by $^1/_2$ again. Whisk in remaining tablespoons of butter. Season with salt and pepper. Reserve.

VEGETABLES

2   Tbs. unsalted butter
6   oz. oyster mushrooms
6   Roma tomatoes, sliced $^1/_4$" thick and oven dried
18   sugar snap peas, blanched

18 golden turnips, peeled and cooked

Salt and pepper to taste

In a hot sauté pan, heat butter. Add mushrooms and cook until tender. Add tomatoes, sugar snap peas, and golden turnips. Season with salt and pepper. Serve immediately.

To Serve

In a hot nonstick pan, sear salmon filets until golden brown on crusted side. Turn and finish in 375°F oven until cooked. Reserve for service.

Place $^1/_2$ cup of leek potato in the center of a large soup bowl. Place 1 piece of salmon on top. Pour 3 ounces of the jus around the bottom of the bowl. Add 3 sugar snap peas, 3 slices of oven dried tomatoes, 3 golden turnips, and 3 oyster mushrooms, and top salmon with herbed prawns. Garnish with chopped chives, Italian parsley, and an orchid.

WARM BANANA-CHOCOLATE BREAD PUDDING WITH CARAMEL SAUCE, KONA COFFEE ICE CREAM, AND BERRIES

(Serves 12)

BANANA BREAD

(Makes a 2-lb. loaf)

$^1/_2$ cup unsalted butter

$^1/_4$ cup sugar

$^1/_4$ cup brown sugar

1 egg, beaten

2 cups cake flour

$^1/_2$ tsp. salt

1 Tbs. baking powder

$^1/_4$ tsp. nutmeg

1 lb. ripe bananas, mashed

1 tsp. vanilla extract

Preheat oven to 350°F. In a small bowl, cream together the butter and sugar and gradually beat in the egg. Mix together flour, salt, baking powder, and nutmeg. Add the mashed bananas to the egg mixture, then fold in the dry ingredients. Blend until smooth. Mix in vanilla extract. Place in a greased 2-pound loaf pan and bake for about 50 minutes or until skewer inserted comes out clean.

CHOCOLATE CUSTARD

$^2/_3$ cup heavy cream

2 lb. bittersweet chocolate

$^1/_4$ cup butter cubes

$2^1/_3$ cups milk

3 eggs, plus 3 egg yolks

$^3/_4$ cup brown sugar

Heat cream to a boil and pour over chocolate and butter. Mix together until smooth. Combine in a saucepan with milk and place over medium heat. Stir until everything has combined thoroughly. Remove from heat. In a separate stainless steel bowl, whisk eggs, egg yolks, and sugar. Add chocolate mixture, whisk, and strain through a fine sieve.

To make the pudding, cut banana bread into 1-inch cubes. Place the cubes in a large bowl and pour in the chocolate custard, enough to cover cubes. Cover with plastic and allow banana bread to soak up the custard (about 30 minutes).

Butter 12 4-ounce tin cups and place in a deep baking pan. Fill cups $^3/_4$ of the way with banana-chocolate custard. Bake at 375°F for about 15 minutes or until custard is set. Let cool for 5 minutes, then remove from tin cups.

CARAMEL SAUCE

$^1/_2$ cup sugar

$^1/_4$ cup heavy cream

Water

Place sugar in a heavy sauce pot. Cover with water and cook over low heat until sugar is dissolved. Increase the heat and boil until sugar caramelizes and turns a deep mahogany brown. Be sure you do not burn the mixture. Gradually pour in the cream; simmer, stirring occasionally until sauce is smooth and thick. Cool and reserve for the banana bread pudding.

KONA COFFEE ICE CREAM

$2^1/_2$ cups heavy cream

1   cup whole milk

$^3/_4$ cup granulated sugar

5   large egg yolks

4   Tbs. espresso powder

$^1/_8$ tsp. ground cinnamon

$^1/_2$ cup Kona coffee, brewed, hot

Candy thermometer

Heat the heavy cream, milk, and $^1/_2$ the sugar in a 3-quart saucepan over medium-high heat. When hot, stir to dissolve the sugar. Bring to a boil.

While the cream is heating, place the egg yolks and the

remaining sugar in the bowl of an electric mixer fitted with a paddle. Beat the eggs on high for 2 to $2^1/_2$ minutes. Scrape down the bowl, then beat on high until slightly thickened and lemon colored ($2^1/_2$ to 3 minutes). (At this point the cream should be boiling. If not, adjust the mixer speed to low and continue to mix until the cream boils. If the eggs are not mixed until the point when the boiling cream is added, they will develop undesirable lumps.)

Pour the boiling cream into the beaten egg yolks and whisk to combine. Return to the saucepan and heat over medium-high heat, stirring constantly. Bring to a temperature of 185°F, in about 1 minute. Remove from the heat and transfer to a 3-quart stainless steel bowl. Place the espresso powder and the ground cinnamon in a separate small bowl. Pour in the hot Kona coffee and stir to dissolve the espresso powder. Pour the Kona coffee and espresso mixture into the cream and egg yolk mixture. Cool in an ice-water bath to a temperature of 40 to 45°F (about 15 minutes).

Freeze the mixture in an ice cream freezer. Following the manufacturer's instructions, transfer the semi-frozen ice cream to a plastic container. Securely cover, then place in the freezer for several hours before serving. Serve within 5 days.

GLAZED BANANA GARNISH

3   bananas, peeled, sliced thin

$^1/_4$ cup brown sugar

Place sliced bananas in a small circle overlapping each other. Sprinkle with brown sugar and place under the broiler to brown (or use a torch).

To Serve

Reheat the chocolate bread pudding in the tin cup until warmed. Place at the center of the plate. Top with glazed bananas and finish with a scoop of Kona coffee ice cream. Drizzle with caramel sauce and garnish with fresh berries and mint.

WINE

Pairing Wine with Chicken

Pairing wine with chicken is easy because there are so many possibilities. Consider how the chicken is prepared and the type of sauce. The sauce will dictate the wine: the heavier the sauce, the heavier the wine. If the chicken is grilled and a heavy sauce is used, consider moving to a red wine such as a Merlot or Barbera.

While the guidelines we have for pairing wines to a dish are helpful, enjoy breaking the rules, and drink the wines you enjoy. Experiment with domestic and international wines with your friends.

STYLE

Lunch Al Fresco

For a relaxed outdoor lunch, do it fresh!

We start with a simple wooden table. For the centerpiece, we select a medium-sized potted flower. Wrap the base in brightly colored fabric and choose cobalt place mats to add a contrasting color.

- Plates with an interesting design add to the festivities.
- Lattice cut-out wooden napkin rings match the wood of the table.
- Keep it simple and elegant with clear stemware.
- Citronella candles are in shallow cups which shield the flames from the wind.

Tropical fruits give a sense of bounty, and your lunch al fresco is ready.

ROXSAND SCOCOS

ROXSAND
PHOENIX, ARIZONA

APPETIZERS

POTATO CAKES WITH SZECHUAN
BLACK BEAN SAUCE

RED WINE AND SHIITAKE
RISOTTO WITH WINTER
VEGETABLE BROTH

ENTRÉES

GRILLED PORK TENDERLOIN
WITH MOLÉ AND PUPUSAS

SALMON WITH GINGER
LEMONGRASS SAUCE

DESSERT

A LOTTA CIACOLATTA

"We can't avoid being influenced by our neighbors. It seems a natural evolution of not just food but social exchanges. Perhaps fusion cuisine is the first step toward a cross-cultural brave new world," says RoxSand Scocos, Executive Chef and co-owner of RoxSand Restaurant and Bar in Phoenix, Arizona. RoxSand has unique ideas regarding fusion cuisine which have generated interest around the culinary world, resulting in her contributions to many cookbooks including *Grand Finales: The Art of the Plated Dessert; Great Women Chefs; Southwest the Beautiful Cookbook; The Great Vegetarian Cookbook; The Gardener Cookbook;* and *Food and Wine* magazine's *America's Best Chefs* and *Superchefs: Signature Recipes from America's New Royalty.*

RoxSand has owned, designed, and worked in her five establishments (as well as wholesale baking company and catering company) over the past fourteen years.

"As a mother, I am very concerned about the future of food choices. Since both the health of our children and the environmental future of the planet are at stake, it is our duty as chefs to send an urgent message about sustainable food choices," says RoxSand. To this end, RoxSand is dedicated to using as close to one-hundred-percent organic products as is possible. RoxSand is on the Board of Overseers of the Chefs Collaborative 2000.

Chef Scocos also understands the importance of solidifying the role of women in the restaurant industry and serves as an executive committee member of the International Association of Women Chefs and Restauranteurs (IAWCR). Through this and other efforts, she promotes the education and advancement of women in the restaurant industry.

PHOTO: *Grilled pork tenderloin with molé and pupusas*

POTATO CAKES WITH SZECHUAN BLACK BEAN SAUCE

(Serves 6 to 8)

POTATO CAKES

6	yellow finn potatoes, shredded
$1/2$	lb. fresh water chestnuts, peeled and shredded
1	Tbs. peanut oil
$1/4$	tsp. salt
$1/4$	tsp. pepper

SALAD

1	jicama, peeled and julienned
1	red bell pepper, julienned
1	yellow bell pepper, julienned
1	green bell pepper, julienned
2	Roma tomatoes, seeded and diced
$1/4$	pineapple, diced

LIME DRESSING

8	cloves garlic
4	jalepeño peppers
$1/2$	cup Nomplac (Asian fish sauce)
$3/4$	cup fresh lime juice (also using zest)
$1/2$	cup rice vinegar
$1/4$	cup basil
$1/4$	cup mint
2	Tbs. sesame oil
2	Tbs. peanut oil

Mix garlic, jalepeños, Nomplac, lime juice, vinegar, basil, and mint in a food processor until well mixed. While still pulsing the mixture, add the oils and emulsify. The dressing will not be very viscous.

BLACK BEAN SAUCE

$1 1/4$	cups sugar

$1/2$	cup light soy sauce
1	Thai chili, coarsely chopped with seeds
4	cloves garlic
$1/4$	cup fermented black beans, rinsed and drained

Caramelize sugar in a heavy-bottomed pot. Once a rich amber color, add soy sauce, chili, garlic, and rinsed beans. Whisk to bring all of the ingredients together. Bring to a boil, then simmer for 15 minutes. Pulse in food processor and strain. Reduce further if necessary.

GARNISH

8	tsp. sesame seeds, toasted
8	tsp. cashews, toasted and chopped

To Serve

"Fry" $1/2$ cup of potato cake mixture in a hot, dry nonstick pan until crispy and golden brown on both sides and potatoes are cooked through. Spoon 1 ounce of black bean sauce onto the center of a warm plate and coat the center of the plate. Place a potato cake on top. Toss $1/2$ cup of the julienned salad vegetables and pineapple together with 1 ounce of the lime dressing. Place a small amount of salad on top of the potato cake, making a mound. Garnish with stemless whole mint leaves and sprinkle a small quantity of toasted sesame seeds and cashews on the rim of the plate.

RED WINE AND SHIITAKE RISOTTO WITH WINTER VEGETABLE BROTH

BROTH

$1/4$	cup olive oil
1	sm. bunch Thyme (tied)
1	leek (white part), diced
1	parsnip, peeled and diced into a brunoise
1	cup rutabaga or turnip, diced into a brunoise
1	onion, diced
1	cup brussel sprout leaves
1	cup tomato concasse julienne
1	cup cannelini beans, cooked and drained

PHOTO: *Red wine and shiitake risotto with winter vegetable broth*

4 cups shiitake mushrooms, chopped

12 cups vegetable stock

Salt and pepper

In a large saucepan, heat oil and sauté the thyme, leek, parsnips, rutabaga, onion, salt and pepper until translucent. Add brussel sprout leaves, tomato concasse, cannelini beans, and shiitake mushroom stems and sauté for 1 minute. Pour in vegetable stock and simmer to infuse flavors. Adjust seasoning.

RISOTTO

$1/2$ cup olive oil

2 Tbs. garlic, chopped

4 cups shiitake caps, sliced

$1^1/2$ lg. onions, diced

$1/2$ cup red wine

2 cups Arborio rice

6 cups boiling mushroom broth

2 cups grated Parmesan cheese

$^1/_4$ lb. butter
Salt and pepper

In a large stock pot over medium heat, add all ingredients and cover the pot to steam. Once ingredients are translucent, remove the cover and gently brown to a rich amber color. Add the red wine to deglaze the pot and reduce by $^3/_4$. Add in rice, sautéing on high heat until all kernels are coated. Begin adding the boiling mushroom broth one ladle at a time, allowing the broth to be absorbed into rice before adding more, stirring continuously. Add grated Parmesan cheese and butter, stirring until well incorporated. Adjust seasoning.

To Serve

The consistency of the risotto will be very creamy. Spoon a cup of the risotto into a deep soup-like plate and ladle 1 cup vegetable and bean broth around it. Garnish with fresh herbs and additional parmesan, if desired. Serve piping hot.

GRILLED PORK TENDERLOIN WITH MOLÉ AND PUPUSAS

(Serves 4)

PORK TENDERLOIN

1   2-lb. tenderloin (cleaned of silverskin and sinew)

Cut pork tenderloin into 6-ounce portions, seasoning with salt and pepper. Grill to order; then slice on the bias.

MOLÉ

6   dried Ancho chilies
$^1/_2$ tsp. cinnamon
$^1/_2$ tsp. black pepper
$^1/_2$ tsp. salt
$^1/_4$ tsp. ground cloves
$^1/_2$ tsp. cumin
$^1/_2$ tsp. cayenne pepper

4   Tbs. cashews
3   oz. lard
4   corn tortillas
4   Tbs. sesame seeds
$1^1/_2$ Roma tomatoes
1   onion, chopped
$^1/_2$ bunch cilantro, chopped
$^1/_2$ tsp. oregano
$1^1/_2$ qt. chicken stock
4   Tbs. raisins

Seed and soak the dried Ancho chilies in hot water, then drain, reserving the soaking water. Mix the dry spices together. Heat the lard in a heavy-bottomed pot. Blanch the tortillas in the lard until crispy; remove and drain. Toast Anchos in the lard; remove and drain. Pour off some of the lard and toast sesame seeds, being careful not to burn them. Sauté the chopped tomato, onion, and cilantro until onions are nicely translucent. Add the spices, raisins, and cashews. Lower the heat and simmer carefully.

In a food processor, add toasted tortillas and chilies. Add some of the reserved chili water to the tortilla-chili mixture while pulsing to make a loose paste. Add to the onion, tomato, and spices. Add the chicken stock and simmer for 1 to 2 hours, reducing by $^1/_3$. Once sauce has cooked down sufficiently, put molé back in the food processor and blend to refine texture. Strain and set aside.

PUPUSA FILLING

$^3/_4$ lb. black beans (cooked through and drained)
1   onion, diced
2   Tbs. garlic, chopped
2   Tbs. curry
$^1/_2$ tsp. cayenne pepper
2   tsp. cumin
2   Tbs. cilantro, chopped
Salt and pepper to taste

In a sauté pan, sauté onion in lard. Add garlic, curry, cayenne pepper, cumin, and cilantro. Place all ingredients in a food processor and pulse until well mixed. Set aside.

MASA FOR PUPUSA

Season masa with salt to taste and moisten with warm water. Knead water in. There is no exact measurement, so a little practice is needed. Roll 1-ounce pieces of masa into balls. Smash down onto pieces of parchment. Place 1 tablespoon of pupusa filling between 2 masa rounds and sandwich together. To cook, heat iron skillet. Use lard and griddle on each side until golden and crispy. Set aside in warm place, covered with a towel.

COLORADO SALSA

1   charred red pepper
1¹/₂ tsp. garlic, chopped
1   Tbs. cilantro, chopped
2   Serrano chilies
1   Pasilia chili, seeded and soaked
1   Ancho chili
¹/₄ tsp. cayenne pepper
¹/₄ tsp. cumin
Salt and pepper

Place all ingredients in a food processor and pulse until mixed.

To Serve

Ladle 2 ounces of molé on a warm plate. Arrange the sliced pork on top of the sauce, fanned out and halfway around the plate, placing a pupusa beside it. Spoon a tablespoon of salsa on the plate and garnish with cilantro.

SALMON WITH GINGER LEMONGRASS SAUCE

(Serves 4)

SALMON BASE SAUCE

1   oz. garlic
1   oz. ginger, thinly sliced
1   oz. lemongrass, cut lengthwise into 2-inch pieces
4   Tbs. Nomplac (Asian fish sauce)
2   cups white wine
2   cups fish fumet

Pan steam the garlic, ginger, and lemongrass. Add the Nomplac, wine, and fish fumet and reduce by ¹/₂. Remove from heat and reserve.

WINE

Cooking with Wine

"I grew up in a family that grew vineyards and made wine, so I take a different approach to cooking with wine. I generally think about the wine I want to have with dinner first, and then I make dinner. If I'm having a Cabernet, I'll use the same Cabernet in cooking. If I'm having a Chardonnay, I'll prepare a meal using that Chardonnay. Using the same wine to prepare the meal allows a consistency of flavors between the wine and the food."

— *Carolyn Wente*

SALMON

4   6-oz. salmon fillets

Fresh sea salt

Fresh black pepper

Lightly season salmon fillet with fresh ground sea salt and black pepper. Sauté in a dry nonstick pan. Remove to a warm plate.

GINGER LEMONGRASS SAUCE

4   oz. lemongrass

2   oz. ginger, sliced

2   oz. garlic (whole cloves), bruised

4   oz. scallions, chopped

4   Tbs. lobster butter

Fresh chervil, chopped

Fresh basil, chopped

Cippolini onions, braised

Chervil garnish

Organic, vine-ripened currant tomatoes, cut into halves

Pan steam lemongrass, ginger, garlic, and scallions, using the base sauce as the liquid medium. Once the essential oils have been released, remove pan lid and add 4 ounces of the base sauce and reduce by $1/2$; add a few tomatoes and cippolini onions; then mount with the lobster butter.

To Serve

Finish sauce with a generous pinch of chopped fresh herbs (chervil and basil). Pour over the top of the salmon without straining out the aromatics. The dish will be somewhat brothy. Arrange braised cippolini onions randomly around perimeter of the fish. Garnish with long wispy chervil and currant tomatoes.

FILLING

3   cups heavy cream

$2/3$ cup sugar

3   Tbs. plus 2 tsp. cocoa

4   oz. mascarpone cheese

$1/3$ cup white crème de menthe

1   tsp. vanilla extract

In a large bowl, whip the heavy cream and sugar to soft peaks. Fold in the cocoa. Fold in the mascarpone cheese, crème de menthe, and vanilla extract. Reserve in refrigerator.

COCOA MERINGUE

7   Tbs. cocoa powder

2   cups powdered sugar

10 oz. egg white

$1^1/3$ cups sugar

Sift cocoa powder and powdered sugar 3 times. In a room-temperature bowl, whip the egg whites to soft peaks. Add sugar to form meringue. Fold in cocoa mixture.

To Serve

Pipe meringue into 3 6-inch rounds with the remainder of meringue piped into sticks for the exterior cake decoration. Place first layer on 8-inch cardboard circle, then spread filling between layers of the piped cocoa meringue and around the top and sides. Then break the "sticks" into 1- to 2-inch lengths and insert all over the cake, making it look like a porcupine. Place them very tightly to avoid seeing any of the underlying cream. Place the cake in the center of a plate, dust the edges of the plate with cocoa powder, and serve.

STYLE

Southwestern Summer

This backyard luncheon is a colorful and festive affair.

Start the celebration with a bright fuschia-colored tablecloth, then add an exotic runner from south of the border. Yellow place mats and alternating yellow and blue ceramic plates add drama to the setting.

The blue-patterned stemware matches the pattern of the napkins and further complements the yellow and blue color scheme.

On the grill or sideboard, arrange maize trivets for a special soup and maize coasters for the glasses.

Flowers are always in order.

Select a decorative maize hamper basket and a bright tapestry to add color, atmosphere, and mystery.

Complete the setting with matching yellow candles and a display of hot peppers from the desert Southwest.

ELIZABETH TERRY

ELIZABETH ON 37TH
SAVANNAH, GEORGIA

APPETIZERS

STUFFED VIDALIA ONIONS
WITH PORK

CRAB AND CRISP POTATO

ENTRÉES

ROASTED GROUPER WITH
SESAME-ALMOND CRUST

GRILLED SIRLOIN WITH FRESH
BLACK-EYED PEA CHILI

DESSERT

CHOCOLATE CINNAMON
APPLE CAKE

"I figured it was just like sewing. You just follow the directions in the book," says Elizabeth Terry about learning to cook as a young bride thirty years ago. Executive Chef and Co-owner of the restaurant Elizabeth on 37th, Chef Terry describes her culinary style as "Coastal Southern, which is not the very spicy cooking of New Orleans and not the farm cooking of the inlands but a full use of garden herbs and vegetables." She and wine steward and husband Michael Terry strive diligently to achieve the goal of refining the experience of Southern dining. "The food should be contemporary but must maintain recognizable, old-fashioned flavors," claims the Executive Chef.

Chef Terry was first smitten by the culinary arts while working in a wine and cheese shop, and later opened her own lunch cafe, Thyme For You. Elizabeth on 37th opened in 1981; its location in an elegant turn-of-the-century mansion reflects the South's simple elegance and sets the stage for stunning regional cooking based on old Southern recipes. Chef Terry extensively researched Savannah cooking of the eighteenth and nineteenth centuries to prepare her menus.

In 1985, *Food & Wine* magazine named Chef Terry one of "25 Hot New American Chefs," and a few years later *Food & Wine* named the restaurant one of the "Top 25 Restaurants in America." *USA Today* ranked Terry as one of the "Top 20 Women Chefs in America" in 1988, and in April 1995, the restaurant received the coveted Ivy Award from *Restaurants & Institutions* magazine. In 1995, Chef Terry was named James Beard Foundation's, "Great Chef of the Southeast." Most recently, Elizabeth and daughter Alexis published *Savannah Seasons, Food and Stories from Elizabeth on 37th.*

PHOTO: *Stuffed Vidalia onions with pork*

STUFFED VIDALIA ONIONS WITH PORK

(Serves 6)

ONION

6   medium-size onions (Vidalia, Walla Walla, or Texas Sweets)

2   oz. (1/4 cup) butter, melted

    Salt and pepper

Preheat the oven to 350°F. Peel the 2 outer layers of the whole onion. Cut 1 inch from each end and scoop out the center with a sharp-edged spoon. Mince and reserve the centers for the stuffing. Place the onions in a shallow baking dish and drizzle with the butter, salt, and pepper. Pour boiling water into the dish until it is about halfway up the sides of the onions. Cover with a lid or foil and bake for 30 minutes until the onions are tender. Remove carefully from the water so the onions do not come apart; drain and set on a buttered baking sheet.

STUFFING

1   lb. bulk spicy sausage

2   cups reserved onion centers, minced

2   Tbs. fresh parsley, minced

1   Tbs. fresh sage, minced

1/4   cup raw milk cheddar, grated

1   tsp. orange peel, minced and grated

1/2   cup white raw milk cheddar

In a medium skillet over high heat, combine the minced onion centers and sausage. Stir and sauté to break up and brown the sausage. Drain and discard the fat and then toss the sausage mixture with orange peel, herbs, and 1/4 cup cheese.

LEMON BUTTER SAUCE

1   Tbs. virgin olive oil

1   tsp. garlic, peeled and minced

1   tsp. shallot, peeled and minced (optional)

1/4   cup white drinking wine or dry white vermouth

1   tsp. grated lemon rind, minced

1   Tbs. lemon juice

1/4   cup heavy cream

3   oz. (6 Tbs.) cold unsalted butter, cubed

In a small sauté pan over high heat, combine and simmer the olive oil, garlic, shallot, white wine, lemon peel, and lemon juice. Reduce to about 2 tablespoons, add the cream and reduce again to 4 tablespoons (this happens very quickly so do not leave the pan). Reduce heat to medium and whisk in the butter, 1 piece at a time, until all butter is melted and the sauce is thick. This will take no longer than a minute. Strain the sauce. This sauce must be kept warm until serving time or it will separate. Do so in a thermos or over a pan of hot water for up to 2 hours before serving.

To Serve

Spoon the stuffing into the cavity of each onion, sprinkle with the additional cheese, and return to the oven to heat and to melt the cheeses (approximately 5 minutes). Serve with lemon butter sauce spooned on each plate and garnish with fresh thyme sprigs.

CRAB AND CRISP POTATO

(Serves 6)

BLUE CRAB

2   lbs. lump back fin blue crab, picked over for shells

1/2   cup Italian parsley, minced

1/4   cup chives, minced

Toss together and set aside until ready to serve.

POTATOES

5   cups potatoes, peeled and 1/2-inch diced

1/4   cup vegetable oil

Preheat oven to 400°F. Soak potatoes in cold water for 10 minutes. Drain and dry well. Toss with the oil and spread on a baking sheet. Bake for 10 minutes until lightly brown and soft. Remove from the oven and set aside. (The potatoes can be baked several hours ahead of time and refrigerated.)

CLASSIC HERB DRESSING

- 2   Tbs. shallot, peeled and minced
- 1   tsp. garlic, peeled and minced
- 2   Tbs. red wine vinegar
- 2   Tbs. fresh basil, minced
- 2   Tbs. fresh tarragon, minced
- 2   Tbs. fresh mint, minced
- $1/4$ tsp. sugar
- $1/2$ tsp. salt
- 1   tsp. fresh cracked pepper
- 2   Tbs. vegetable oil
- $1/4$ cup extra virgin olive oil
- 2   Tbs. hot water

In the bowl of a food processor, combine the shallot, garlic, vinegar, herbs, sugar, salt, and pepper. With the motor running, slowly pour in the oils. Continue processing to pour in the hot water. Set aside to combine the flavors.

To Serve

Just before serving, toss the dressing with the crab, parsley and chives. Return potatoes to the oven to heat through and crisp for about 5 minutes. Toss with the crab and serve immediately.

ROASTED GROUPER WITH SESAME-ALMOND CRUST

(Serves 6)

GROUPER

- 6   6-oz. boneless and skinless black grouper filets, $1/2$-inch thick

GROUPER MARINADE

- 2   Tbs. sesame oil
- 2   Tbs. vegetable oil
- 2   Tbs. lemon juice
- 2   Tbs. water
- 1   egg, beaten
- $1/4$ tsp. salt
- $1/4$ tsp. pepper

PHOTO: *Roasted grouper with sesame-almond crust*

- 1   tsp. hot chili sauce

Preheat the oven to 425ºF. In a medium bowl, combine the sesame oil, vegetable oil, lemon juice, water, beaten egg, salt, pepper, and chili sauce. Set aside.

SESAME-ALMOND CRUMBS

- 1   cup stoned wheat thins or other crisp wheat cracker, crushed
- $1/2$ cup Asiago cheese, grated
- $1/4$ cup almonds, toasted
- 2   Tbs. sesame seeds, toasted
- $1/4$ cup Italian parsley, minced
- 2   Tbs. tarragon, minced
- $1/2$ tsp. cracked black pepper

Combine the wheat thins, cheese, almonds, sesame seeds, parsley, tarragon, and pepper in the bowl of a food processor and process to a crumb. Set aside.

- 2   Tbs. butter, melted
- 2   Tbs. extra virgin olive oil

Dip the fish fillet in the marinade, then in the crumbs. Place on a buttered, shallow baking pan, making sure the fillets do not touch each other. Combine the butter and olive oil and drizzle over the fish, then roast in the oven for 20 minutes until browned and cooked through.

PEANUT SAUCE

- 1   cup peanut butter
- 2   Tbs. soy sauce

2 tsp. hot chili sauce

$^1/_4$ cup lemon juice

2 Tbs. garlic, minced

$^1/_2$ cup water

Blend all ingredients in a food processor until mixture reaches the consistency of a thick sauce (milkshake thickness). Add up to another $^1/_2$ cup water to reduce sauce to desired thickness.

SQUASH AND ZUCCHINI

3 zucchini

3 yellow squash

3 Tbs. olive oil

6 Tbs. Asiago cheese, grated

Salt and pepper to taste

Cut zucchini and squash into medallions and alternate layers in a baking dish. Brush with olive oil and season with salt and pepper. Sprinkle Asiago cheese over the zucchini and squash medallions and place in a 425°F oven for 10 minutes. Remove from the oven and serve hot.

To Serve

Spoon peanut sauce onto the center of plate and place a grouper fillet on top. Place a spoonful of the zucchini and squash on the plate and garnish with fresh fennel sprigs. Serve immediately.

Wine Recommendation:

Chalone Pinot Blanc

GRILLED SIRLOIN WITH FRESH BLACK-EYED PEA CHILI

(Serves 6)

SIRLOIN

6 6-oz. well-trimmed steaks, strip or tenderloin

BLACK-EYED PEA CHILI

2 Tbs. peanut oil

1 Tbs. chili powder

$^1/_4$ cup green pepper, minced, seeds discarded

$^1/_4$ cup water

1 15-oz. can black-eyed peas, rinsed

2 cups fresh garden tomatoes, diced, seeds discarded

$^1/_4$ cup green onion, minced

In a large skillet over high heat, add the oil, chili powder, and green pepper. Sauté 1 minute, lower the heat to medium, then stir in the water and black-eyed peas and simmer 5 minutes. Add the diced tomato, stir well, then add the green onion. Remove from the heat and let cool. Serve at room temperature.

MARINADE

2 Tbs. vegetable oil

2 Tbs. fresh cracked black pepper

1 Tbs. curry powder

2 Tbs. fresh lime juice

Light the grill. In a bowl, whisk together the oil, pepper, curry powder, and lime juice. Brush the steaks with the marinade and allow to rest 15 minutes, turning once. Grill the steaks 3 min-

WINE

Describing Wine

When trying to characterize a wine, start with the color: red, white, or rosé. Next, is it dry or sweet? The sweetness will help determine which foods you serve with the wine. When the wine is in your mouth, consider its weight and feel. Is it light, medium bodied, or really heavy and mouth filling? The weight and feel are important when matching a wine with food. The important thing, of course, is the flavor itself. Wine flavors range through many of the food smells and tastes with which we are familiar. Does the wine taste like a tree fruit, such as apricot, peach or pear? Does it taste like blackberries, blueberries, or raspberries? Since wine is made from grapes, it naturally will have flavors reminiscent of fruit.

utes per side, turning only once. Remove steaks from the grill and allow the meat to rest 5 minutes before serving.

To Serve

Place steaks on a plate and spoon the black-eyed pea chili over the top. Serve with crusty bread and green salad.

Chef's Note

The curry powder and the chili powder combine to give the steaks quite a zip and a true backyard flavor. A 2$^1/_2$ pound, well-trimmed, center-cut strip or tenderloin roast may be rubbed whole with the marinade and roasted in a 375°F oven for 35 minutes before slicing and serving.

CHOCOLATE CINNAMON APPLE CAKE

(Serves 6 to 8)

CINNAMON APPLE CAKE

1   8-inch springform pan, buttered and floured
1$^1/_2$ cups cake flour
$^1/_2$ cup whole wheat pastry flour
1$^1/_2$ tsp. baking soda
$^1/_2$ tsp. salt
$^1/_2$ tsp. cinnamon
$^1/_2$ cup brown sugar, firmly packed
$^1/_2$ cup white sugar
$^1/_2$ cup vegetable oil
2   eggs
4   tart Granny Smith apples, peeled, large grated, then core discarded
$^1/_2$ cup unsweetened baking chocolate, grated (1$^1/_2$ oz.)
1   tsp. vanilla

Preheat the oven to 350°F. In a bowl, sift the cake flour, pastry flour, baking soda, salt, and cinnamon. Set aside. Using a cheese grater, grate the apples using the largest size hole possible.

In the bowl of a mixer combine the oil and sugars, then add the eggs 1 at a time while beating. Beat mixture approximately 4 minutes until fluffy. Fold in the sifted dry ingredients, grated apple, chocolate, and vanilla. Pour batter into the prepared pan and bake for 40 minutes until a knife inserted in the center comes out clean. Cool on a rack. Frost with chocolate topping.

CHOCOLATE FROSTING.

4   Tbs. sugar
1   cup cream
6   oz. bittersweet chocolate, chopped
4   oz. butter, cut into small cubes
2   tsp. vanilla

In a medium saucepan over medium heat, stir the sugar and cream together. Bring mixture to a boil, lower the heat and simmer for 3 minutes, no longer. Place the chocolate and the butter in a medium bowl and pour in the sweetened cream, stirring continuously until the butter and chocolate are melted. Stir in the vanilla and set aside to cool. Pour and spread over the completely cool cake. Refrigerate briefly to set the frosting if the kitchen is warm. Serve at room temperature.

STYLE

Let Me Count the Ways

For that special occasion when you pop the question or say you want to spend another twenty years together, keep it simple and dramatic. Irish lace covers a black tablecloth, and brass chargers hold the white plates. Candies in a heart-shaped glass bowl add a whimsical touch. Sprinkle clear glass gems around the table for more fun, and decorate the napkins with a flower. Is there a special gift? Make it part of the setting. Candles complete the mood for this intimate dinner of love.

GUILLERMO VELOSO

YUCA

MIAMI BEACH, FLORIDA

APPETIZERS

PIONONO DE CAMARON

GRILLED MARINATED
PORTOBELLO MUSHROOMS
STUFFED WITH VEGETARIAN
PAELLA

ENTRÉES

SEARED FILLET OF CHILEAN
SEA BASS OVER BONIATO
GINGER MASH AND A LIGHT
ROASTED CORN AND LOBSTER
BROTH

PUMPKIN SEED-CRUSTED AND
PAN-ROASTED VEAL RIB CHOP
OVER PURPLE POTATO AND
LOBSTER MASH WITH A RIOJA,
SHALLOT, AND ROASTED CORN
JUS

DESSERT

TROPICAL FRUIT FANDANGO

A New York City native, born to parents of Spanish and Puerto Rican descent, Executive Chef Guillermo Veloso of Yuca in Miami Beach, Florida, has extensively used his Latin heritage to bring style, flair, and flavor to his menu.

Chef Veloso was just six credits short of receiving a degree in archaeology when he realized that cooking was his first love. Shortly thereafter, Veloso graduated from the prestigious culinary academy Johnson & Wales University in Providence, Rhode Island. Chef Veloso has worked in the kitchens of various restaurants in New Jersey, including the 500-room Radisson Hotel in Newark, where he held the position of Executive Sous Chef. In 1990, Veloso moved to the warmer climate of South Florida, where he worked for a year as Sous Chef at the Hotel St. Michel in Coral Gables. Chef Veloso then worked alongside Nuevo Cubano Chef Douglas Rodriguez (a 1995 America's Rising Star Chef) at Yuca. Several years later, upon Chef Rodriguez's resignation, Veloso took over as Executive Chef of Yuca's kitchen.

Chef Veloso has maintained Yuca's reputation for excellence and innovation, earning it a ranking of "Exceptional" from the *Miami Herald* and a rating of among the best by South Florida's Critic's Choice. In 1995, Veloso was an invited chef at the first Latin Chef Sizzle at Patria Restaurant in New York City. He has been featured on CNN and *Great Chefs of the South*, both in 1996.

Chef Veloso plans to keep exploring his Latin heritage to bring these culinary treasures to the American public.

PHOTO: *Tropical fruit fandango*

GUILLERMO VELOSO

PIONONO DE CAMARON
(Serves 4)

SHRIMP

2 lbs. shrimp, peeled, deveined, and roughly cut

2 tomatoes, diced

1 onion, diced

4 cloves garlic, minced

$1^1/_2$ cups white wine

$^1/_2$ cup sofrito

$^1/_4$ lb. whole butter

1 bunch fresh basil, cut into a chiffonade

Sauté shrimp with tomato, onions, and garlic until shrimp are half-cooked. Remove shrimp and deglaze with white wine and sofrito. Reduce by half. After reduction, finish with butter. Return shrimp to pan and add basil.

2 sweet plantains

$^1/_4$ cup grated manchego cheese

4-inch metal ring mold

Egg wash

Slice plantains $^1/_4$-inch thick on a mandoline, lengthwise. Deep fry until the slices are just golden (they can also be sautéed). Form 2 strips per order into the 4-inch metal ring mold (or with toothpicks). Fill the mold with the shrimp mixture and brush the top with the egg wash. Sprinkle with the manchego cheese and bake for 20 minutes in a 350°F oven.

SHERRY SAUCE

4 shallots, minced

2 cups Spanish sherry

$^1/_4$ cup sherry vinegar

1 vanilla bean, split and scraped

Pinch of saffron

$^1/_4$ cup cream

$^1/_2$ lb. whole butter

Lightly sauté shallots until translucent. Deglaze with sherry and sherry vinegar. Add vanilla and saffron and reduce by $^1/_2$. Add cream. Reduce by $^1/_2$ again. Whisk in butter until mixed well.

To Serve

Place a shrimp-filled mold in the center of a plate and spoon the sherry sauce around. Garnish with chopped chives.

GRILLED MARINATED PORTOBELLO MUSHROOMS STUFFED WITH VEGETARIAN PAELLA
(Serves 6)

PORTOBELLOS

6 lg. Portobello caps

$^1/_4$ cup balsamic vinegar

1 Tbs. garlic, chopped

$^1/_4$ cup olive oil

1 bunch basil, julienned

Salt and pepper to taste

Remove stems from Portobellos (reserve for stock). Marinate caps in remaining ingredients. Grill on a barbecue grill or broil in broiler oven until tender.

VEGETABLE STOCK

$^1/_2$ cup olive oil

2 carrots, diced

1 bunch leeks, sliced

1 cup mushroom stems (Portobello)

3 tomatoes, quartered

4 heads of garlic, peeled and cut in half

2 onions, quartered

2 bunches of celery, diced

2 gal. cold water

4 bay leaves

2 cups of white wine

1 Tbs. peppercorns

In a stock pot over high heat, heat olive oil. Add vegetables and sauté. Stir continuously so as to caramelize. Cover with 2 gallons of cold water and bring to a boil. Add bay leaves, wine, and peppercorns. Simmer for 1 hour. Season to taste. If desired, tomato paste may be added for a thicker consistency.

VEGETARIAN PAELLA

$1/2$ cup olive oil

2   tomatoes, diced

1   onion, diced

$1/4$ cup garlic, minced

2   pinches saffron threads

4   cups Arborio rice

10 cups vegetable stock

1   cup portobello mushrooms, quartered

1   cup asparagus, sliced

1   cup zucchini, diced

1   cup yellow squash, diced

$1/2$ cup red peppers, diced

$1/2$ cup broccoli florets

In a saucepan, heat olive oil. Add tomatoes, onion, and garlic. Sauté until onions are translucent. Add saffron. Stir in rice until coated in oil. Over medium heat, ladle stock over rice until covered. Stirring continuously, let rice absorb liquid. Add liquid in batches, letting rice absorb each time, until all stock is used or until rice is cooked (preferably slightly al dente). Add uncooked vegetables to rice and stir well. Reserve rice.

To Serve

Stuff caps with a large spoonful of paella. Place in a preheated 350°F oven for 10 minutes. Serve hot immediately. Garnish with shaved Parmesan or manchego, and serve with Idiazabal- or goat-cheese-flavored oil and warm bread.

SEARED FILLET OF CHILEAN SEA BASS OVER BONIATO GINGER MASH AND A LIGHT ROASTED CORN AND LOBSTER BROTH

(Serves 4 to 6)

SEA BASS

1   3-lb. Chilean sea bass fillet (substitute grouper or snapper)

Salt and pepper

Fresh herbs

Season fillet with salt, pepper, and fresh herbs. Sear on both sides in a hot pan and finish in a 250°F oven for 6 to 7 minutes.

BONIATO GINGER MASH POTATOES

2   lbs. boniato potatoes (Cuban sweet potatoes) or substitute regular sweet potatoes

3   cups milk

2   oz. fresh ginger, minced

2   bulbs lemongrass, minced

$1/2$ qt. heavy cream

$1/2$ lb. butter

$1/2$ bunch scallions

Boil the boniato potatoes in milk until tender and drain off excess water. In a large, heavy-bottomed saucepan add heavy cream, butter, lemongrass, ginger, and scallions. Reduce by $1/2$. Use the reduction when mashing with the boniatoes. Mash until well mixed.

LOBSTER BROTH

4   cups rich lobster stock

1   pinch saffron or Bijol

1   cup fresh roasted corn kernels

Salt and pepper to taste

Simmer the lobster stock, corn, and saffron together for several minutes. Season with salt and pepper, and blend with stick blender. Keep warm for service.

GARNISH

1   bunch fresh chives

1   mango, sliced

1   papaya, sliced

To Serve

Place the mashed boniato in the center of a large bowl and ladle the broth around the mash. Place the roasted bass on top of the mash. Garnish with fresh chives, a slaw of red cabbage, and either mango or papaya slices.

GUILLERMO VELOSO

PUMPKIN SEED-CRUSTED AND PAN-ROASTED VEAL RIB CHOP OVER PURPLE POTATO AND LOBSTER MASH WITH A RIOJA, SHALLOT, AND ROASTED CORN JUS
(Serves 4)

PHOTO: *Pumpkin seed-crusted and pan-roasted veal rib chop over purple potato and lobster mash with a Rioja, shallot, and roasted corn jus*

CHOPS
4   veal rib chops, bone in, frenched

PUMPKIN SEED CRUST
$^1/_2$ lb. pumpkin seeds
3   Tbs. cumin seeds
4   Tbs. olive oil
Salt and pepper

In a spice grinder, grind cumin and pumpkin seeds and set aside. Crust each veal chop heavily with ground cumin and pumpkin seeds, salt, and pepper. Sear quickly in hot olive oil. Remove from oil and place in an oven-safe pan. Finish to desired temp in the oven, 6 to 7 minutes for medium rare or longer for desired doneness.

PURPLE POTATO AND LOBSTER MASH
1   lb. purple Peruvian potatoes
1   Tbs. butter
3   cups rich lobster stock from shells
$^1/_2$ cup heavy cream
1   Tbs. tomato paste
1   tomato, diced
2   Maine lobsters or Florida lobsters, cooked and meat medium diced (save shells)
$^1/_4$ bunch cilantro, chopped
Salt and pepper

Boil the potatoes, starting in cold, salted water, until cooked. Dry them in the oven. Once dry, mash the potatoes with a hand masher. Set aside to cool. Take the lobster stock and reduce with salt, pepper, tomatoes, heavy cream, and butter. Reheat the mash with fresh lobster, lobster cream, and cilantro.

Mash all ingredients together with a hand masher. Add the cilantro last so it does not lose its color, texture, or flavor.

CORN JUS
3   cloves garlic, sliced
8   lg. shallots, julienne
1   qt. Rioja wine
$1^1/_2$ cups corn kernels, roasted
2   cups demi-glace
1   bunch scallions, chopped
2   Tbs. whole butter

Sauté garlic and shallots until tender; deglaze with Rioja and reduce by $^1/_2$. Add the corn and demi-glace and reduce to desired consistency. Add scallions. Season with salt, pepper, and a little whole butter.

To Serve
Place a generous spoonful of the corn jus in the bottom of a large shallow bowl. Place a veal chop on top of the corn jus. Place a spoonful of the purple potato and lobster mash on the plate and garnish with lobster antennae and fins from the tail. Serve immediately.

TROPICAL FRUIT FANDANGO
(Serves 4)

TROPICAL FRUIT
$^1/_2$ cup carambola, diced

$^1/_2$ cup mango, diced

$^1/_2$ cup strawberry, diced

$^1/_2$ cup papaya, diced

$^1/_2$ cup passion fruit, scooped

$^1/_2$ cup kiwi, diced

$^1/_2$ cup pineapple, diced

Dice the fruit and place in a large nonreactive bowl. Set aside.

SYRUP

1 cup anejo (aged) rum

1 lime, zested

1 lemon, zested

2 star anise

2 cinnamon sticks

$^1/_2$ cup sugar (scented by vanilla beans)

In medium-sized saucepan, steep the ingredients together for several minutes until sugar dissolves and cinnamon sticks open up. Strain syrup and set aside to cool. Pour the cooled syrup over the diced fruits and allow to macerate.

CARAMEL WHIPPED CREAM

1 can condensed milk

3 cups stiff heavy cream

$^1/_2$ cup macadamia nuts, chopped

$^1/_4$ cup macadamia nuts, chopped (for garnish)

Remove the label from 1 can of condensed milk and place the can in a pot of boiling water. Allow to boil for 40 to 50 minutes. Remove from boiling water and allow to cool. Once cooled, open the can. The condensed milk will have caramelized. In a chilled bowl, whip the heavy cream until stiff peaks form. Fold in the caramelized condensed milk. Once completely incorporated, fold in the chopped macadamia nuts.

To Serve

Spoon macerated fruit into a margarita glass. Top with a generous spoonful of the caramel whipped cream and sprinkle with chopped macadamia nuts for garnish.

WINE

Pairing Wine with Veal and Dessert

Veal is a white meat, so consider pairing it with a white wine. It is lighter and therefore you can match a Chardonnay or even a fuller bodied Sauvignon Blanc. When you start to add sauces or a crust on the veal chop, consider a heavier red wine such as a Pinot Noir or even a fruity style Zinfandel.

When pairing wines with dessert, think about the sweetness of the dessert. You want a wine that is sweeter than the dessert itself because a wine less sweet will taste sour or bitter.

STYLE

Fandango

It's African in origin and as colorful and lively as the music from which it got its name. For our Fandango setting, find a light and airy spot and build the table setting in yellows and blues to reflect the vibrancy and beauty of the Caribbean. To a basic white tablecloth, add yellow runners, blue chargers, and white place settings with a fanciful flower pattern to create a setting for laughter and friendship. Match the flatware to the plates, the napkins to the runners, and the glasses to the chargers for a bright, coordinated look. Candles are festive and flowers floating in water suggest the clear blue of the Caribbean. More flowers and green plants are always in order to bring nature to your table. Add fruit punch in a clear glass pitcher for an especially inviting color and a thirst quencher for a hot afternoon.

PATRICIA WILLIAMS

RESTAURANT CHARLOTTE
AT THE MILLENIUM BROADWAY HOTEL
NEW YORK, NEW YORK

APPETIZER

BRAISED CALAMARI AND HERB
SALAD

CARROT RISOTTO WITH MAINE
SHRIMP

ENTRÉES

CURRIED SALMON

HERB RACK OF LAMB WITH
LEMON-THYME SAUCE RISOTTO
AND HONEY-GLAZED CARROTS

DESSERT

ANGEL FOOD CAKE WITH FRESH
BERRIES

"We are very conscious that most of our guests are seeking to avoid heavy meals. Our goal is to provide them with light, satisfying fare that will challenge their taste buds," says Patricia Williams, Executive Chef of Restaurant Charlotte in the Millennium Broadway in New York City. Texas-born of Cherokee/Mexican heritage, this former ballerina for the New York City Opera Ballet flawlessly choreographs a talented team of twenty, producing her innovative blend of traditional American and Southwestern cuisine with an emphasis on flavor and simple presentation. Chef Williams is constantly experimenting, taking full advantage of seasonal fruits and vegetables, and forgoing heavy sauces for a lighter style of cuisine.

After the culmination of her career at the New York City Opera Ballet, Chef Williams spent three months in France observing food preparation and surveying vineyards before returning to attend the New York Restaurant School.

Upon graduation, Chef Williams gained invaluable management experience through her work in the kitchens of 150 Wooster (she opened the restaurant as its first chef), Sarabeth's Kitchen, the eclectic Quilted Giraffe, and Arizona 206. It was at Arizona 206 that Williams perfected her signature blend of traditional American and Southwestern cuisine. In 1991, Chef Williams joined the staff at the notable New York restaurant The Supper Club. Two years later she accepted the position of Executive Chef at Restaurant Charlotte, and has received accolades from *Gourmet* magazine and gained a loyal following.

PHOTO: *Herb rack of lamb with lemon-thyme sauce risotto and honey-glazed carrots*

BRAISED CALAMARI AND HERB SALAD

(Serves 6)

2	Tbs. shallots, minced
1	Tbs. garlic, minced
2	cups red wine
5	bay leaves
1	qt. chicken stock
$1/2$	Tbs. salt
1	tsp. pepper
2	sprigs thyme
2	sprigs oregano
$2^1/2$	lbs. calamari, cut into rings

In a large sauce pot over medium heat, add minced shallots, minced garlic, red wine, and bay leaves and reduce by $1/2$. Once reduced, add the chicken stock, salt, pepper, thyme, and oregano and cook for 10 minutes. Next, add the calamari and cook for 15 minutes until tender. Do not boil. After 15 minutes remove from heat, strain out the calamari and other ingredients and reserve. Return the calamari braising liquid to the heat and reduce by $1/2$; remove from heat and reserve.

VINAIGRETTE

$1/2$	cup calamari braising liquid
$1/2$	cup red wine vinegar
$1/2$	cup balsamic vinegar
3	Tbs. garlic confit (whole peeled garlic cloves cooked in olive oil until tender and puréed in a food processor)
2	cups olive oil
	Salt and pepper to taste

In a medium-sized, nonreactive bowl add the cooled braising liquid, vinegars, and garlic confit. Slowly whisk olive oil in with other ingredients. Adjust seasonings.

MESCLUN SALAD

$1/2$	lb. mesclun
	A mixture of herb leaves: chives-batonettes, chervil, basil, tarragon, parsley, and cilantro

Wash and dry greens well. Toss mesclun and herbs together and set aside.

To Serve

Combine the braised calamari with mesclun and herb mixture and dress lightly with the vinaigrette. Place on individual salad plates.

CARROT RISOTTO WITH MAINE SHRIMP

(Serves 6)

LEMONGRASS GINGER CREAM

2	cups heavy cream
1	stalk lemongrass, coarsely chopped
3	Tbs. ginger, minced

In a heavy-bottomed sauce pot simmer the lemongrass and ginger in the heavy cream for 15 minutes. Reduce heat to low and steep for 15 minutes; strain the liquid and keep warm for service.

CARROT RISOTTO

1	lb. Arborio rice
2	oz. butter, clarified
1	Tbs. shallots, minced
$1/2$	Tbs. garlic, minced
2	qt. chicken stock
$1/4$	lb. butter
2	Tbs. salt
2	cups fresh carrot juice
1	lb. Maine shrimp (25 pieces)
	Chives or chervil sprigs (for garnish)

In a medium-sized stock pot, heat the chicken stock. Poach the shrimp in the stock for about 3 minutes. Remove the shrimp from the stock, chill, and peel. Sauté the shallots and garlic in the butter until tender. Add the rice and coat thoroughly. Begin adding the hot chicken stock slowly, ladle by ladle. Do not add more stock until all has been absorbed. Continue until all the chicken stock has been added. Proceed with the lemongrass ginger cream in the same way. At this point, begin tasting the risotto and add the carrot juice. The risotto should be al dente, not creamy in the middle. Add the shrimp and stir. Place risotto in the center of each plate and garnish with fresh chives or chervil.

CURRIED SALMON
(Serves 6)

SALMON
6   7-oz. salmon fillets

MUSTARD SALMON COATING
1   cup Coleman's dry mustard
$^1/_2$ cup sugar
$^1/_4$ cup water

Mix ingredients together and set aside.

SALMON HERB COATING
4   oz. mustard seed
4   oz. coriander seed
4   oz. fennel seed
4   oz. cumin seed
2   tsp. cloves
2   oz. black peppercorns

Place all ingredients in a spice grinder and grind well.

VEGETABLES
2   oz. butter, clarified
1   med. onion, finely diced
1   Tbs. garlic, minced
3   oz. white wine
$1^1/_2$ Tbs. curry powder
1   cup coconut milk
1   qt. chicken stock
2   qt. cauliflower florets
2   Yukon gold potatoes, diced
3   carrots, diced

In a large saucepan, sauté the diced onion in clarified butter until soft. Add the minced garlic and sauté until soft. Next, add the white wine, curry powder, coconut milk, and chicken stock and let simmer for 15 minutes. Add cauliflower florets. When the florets are partially cooked, add the diced Yukon gold potatoes and carrots. Season with salt and pepper. Cook until vegetables are tender and remove.

To Serve
Sauté the salmon and place in oven for 5 minutes. Take out of the oven and brush with mustard then sprinkle lightly with herb mixture. Place in 450°F oven for 5 minutes. Place curried vegetables in a bowl and top with the salmon.

HERB RACK OF LAMB WITH LEMON-THYME SAUCE RISOTTO AND HONEY-GLAZED CARROTS
(Serves 8)

RACKS OF LAMB
2   racks of lamb

BARLEY RISOTTO
3   Tbs. butter
3   Tbs. shallots, minced
1   Tbs. garlic, minced
1   lb. barley
1   cup white wine
4   cups hot chicken stock
$^1/_4$ cup heavy cream
1   Tbs. garlic confit (whole peeled garlic cloves cooked in olive oil until tender and pureed)
2   Tbs. butter

Salt and pepper to taste

In a large, heavy-bottomed saucepan, sauté the butter, shallots, and garlic until translucent. Add the barley, making sure the grains are well coated. Add the wine in stages, making sure the wine is reduced before adding more. Slowly add the hot chicken stock, stirring until all the stock has been absorbed before adding more. Add the heavy cream, garlic confit, and butter. Make sure the ingredients are mixed well. Season with salt and pepper to taste and keep warm.

LEMON THYME SAUCE

1 Tbs. shallots

1/2 Tbs. garlic

3/4 cup lemon juice

3 oz. honey

21/2 cups white wine

1/2 gal. lamb glace

In a heavy-bottomed stock pot, add shallots, garlic, lemon juice, honey, and white wine and reduce to a glace. Stir in the lamb glace and infuse with the lemon thyme.

MUSTARD LAMB COATING

1 cup Coleman's dry mustard

1/2 cup sugar

1/4 cup water

Mix ingredients together and set aside.

COATING FOR LAMB

11/2 cup bread crumbs

4 Tbs. coriander, ground, toasted

3 Tbs. cardamom, ground, toasted

11/2 Tbs. ginger, ground

Mix ingredients together in a bowl large enough to dredge the racks of lamb. Set aside.

HONEY-GLAZED CARROTS

1 lb. baby carrots, peeled and blanched until tender

2 Tbs. butter

1 Tbs. honey

1/2 tsp. ginger, ground

1/2 tsp. coriander, ground

1/2 tsp. cardamom, ground

In a pot of boiling water, blanch the baby carrots until tender. Remove carrots from heat and water, and reserve. In a sauté pan over medium heat, add butter and honey. Let the pan begin to slightly darken, and add a pinch of ground ginger, coriander, and cardamom. Add carrots to the pan, making sure

PHOTO: *Angel food cake with fresh berries*

they are well coated. Remove from heat.

To Serve

Sear the lamb that has been seasoned with salt and pepper and place in the oven; cook at 450°F about 10 minutes. Take the lamb out and brush with mustard and dredge in seasoned bread crumbs. Place in the oven for 5 minutes. In the meantime, sauce the plate with risotto in the center. Remove racks from the oven, skin the rack in half, and place interlocking the bones on top of the risotto. Place glazed carrots in front of the risotto and lamb and garnish with lemon thyme. Serve immediately.

Wine Recommendation:
Concannon Vineyard Central Coast Petite Sirah

ANGEL FOOD CAKE WITH FRESH BERRIES
(Serves 6 to 8)

ANGEL FOOD CAKE

1 cup flour

1/3 cup super fine sugar

1 pinch salt

2 sheets of paper

1¹/₂ cups egg whites

1 tsp. fresh lemon juice

Several drops almond extract

1 tsp. cream of tartar

1¹/₂ tsp. vanilla extract

1 tsp. cold water

1 cup super fine sugar

Seasonal fresh berries

Use a 64-ounce bundt pan. Cut a piece of parchment paper to the size of the bottom of the cake pan and place in the pan; do not grease. Preheat oven to 425°F.

Sift flour onto a sheet of paper. Sift 3 more times, working back and forth between 2 sheets of paper, and set aside. In a clean, room-temperature bowl, beat egg whites on medium-low speed until foamy. Slowly add lemon juice, almond extract, cream of tartar, vanilla extract, and water to egg whites. Increase speed and beat until whites are nearly stiff. Reduce speed and beat sugar in, 2 tablespoons at a time. Beat until peaks are stiff but not dry. Turn mixer off.

Sift ¹/₄ flour mixture onto whites; fold in gently. Repeat 3 more times, adding remaining flour. Gently transfer batter to prepped pan. Run a knife through batter to eliminate air pockets and gently smooth top.

Bake in 425°F oven until cake is lightly golden and springs back (which should take about 45 minutes). Remove cake from oven and invert it, still in pan; hang over neck of funnel or bottle. Let cake hang until completely cooled. Run knife tip around sides to loosen cake; unmold. Cut with separate knife.

To Serve

Place a slice of the cake in the center of a plate and arrange seasonal berries around.

WINE

Mèthode Champagnois

Wente Vineyards produces a Mèthode Champagnoise sparkling wine that starts with a blend of Chardonnay, Pinot Noir, and Pinot Blanc grapes, to which is added yeast and sugar to start a secondary fermentation. The wine is bottled with the sugar and yeast, then sealed, trapping the carbon dioxide given off as the yeast converts the sugar into alcohol. After the yeast eats all the sugar, it comes to rest in the bottle, breaking down and imparting a rich, toasty flavor to the sparkling wine. The bottle is kept neck-down in an A-frame rack. The yeast is removed by freezing the bottle and removing the cap. The pressure from the trapped carbon dioxide gas forces the frozen plug of yeast and wine out of the bottle. The bottle is corked, aged, and sent to market.

To complement fresh berries, select a late-harvest Riesling (picked later in the season, giving it a higher sugar content). With a light, airy dessert such as angel food cake, try a sparkling wine. The effervescence will be a nice finish to the meal, with the bubbles cleansing your palate.

STYLE

Spring Fling

This festive setting brings eternal spring—no matter what time of year you greet your friends.

Start with a white tablecloth and add place mats, plates, and glasses in soft pastel floral and spring patterns. Select two napkins of different colors to create a layered look and green stemware to remind us of mother earth. Cover the bases of plants with similar but not identical napkins to give an eclectic and lighthearted feeling to the room. A simple potted plant brings spring to the table, a colorful fruit drink adds flavor, and candles, day or night, augment the mood.

★ INDEX

*Italicized entries are the names of plates as they appear in the chef's menus.

Italicized entries are the names of plates as they appear in the chef's menus

S

Saffron lima beans, for salmon on seared rapini, 29

Saffron marjoram chardonnay sauce, for seared filet of sea bass with macadamia peanut crust, 45

Sake-poached cod, with quinoa and shiitakes, 38

Salad, braised calamari and herb, 112

Salad, for potato cakes with szechuan black bean sauce, 92

Salad, grilled Caesar, 12

Salad, lentil and basmati with coriander oil, 28

Salad, red onion-cucumber, with aged balsamic vinaigrette, 61

Salad, soft herb with roasted egg plant cannelloni, 76

Salmon base sauce, for salmon with lemongrass ginger sauce, 95–96

Salmon herb coating, for curried salmon, 113

Salmon, on seared rapini with saffron lima bean broth, 29–30

Salmon, with ginger lemongrass sauce, 95

Salmon, curried, 113

Salmon, sockeye martini, with nectarine-peanut salsa, 20

Sea bass, seared with lemon-thyme hoisin sauce, and macadamia-peanut crust, 45

Sea bass, seared, over boniato ginger mash and a light roasted corn and lobster broth, 107

Sea scallops, carpaccio style, with exotic fruit relish, lime, sesame oil, and chives, 43

Sea scallops, grilled, with Maine lobster–sweet corn pancake, 59–60

Seared fillet of Chilean sea bass over boniato ginger mash, and a light roasted corn, lobster broth, 107

Sesame ice cream, with chilled summer fruit soup, 23

Sesame lavosh, for pizza with apple-onion marmalade, oven-dried tomatoes, and herb goat cheese, 58

Sesame-almond crumbs, for crust of roasted grouper, 101

Shallot-mustard vinaigrette, for grilled vegetable sandwich with new potato salad, 61

Shell bean minestre, 5

Sherry sauce, for pionono de cameron, 106

Sherry, mustard, and pink pepper corn vinaigrette, with herbed, chicken breast, 84

Shrimp, for pionono de cameron, 106

Shrimp, with grits cakes, country ham and "redeye" vinaigrette, 5-6

Sirloin, grilled, with fresh black-eyed pea chili, 102

Skate salad, with local tomatoes, sorrel, and caper vinaigrette, 26

Snow peas, for spice-crusted pork tenderloin, 37

Sockeye salmon martini, with nectarine-peanut salsa, 20

Spice-crusted pork tenderloin, 37

Spiced quince, for fruit compote, soaked in Earl Grey Tea, 39

Spinach layer, for herbed eggplant, potato, and tomato torte, with ancho chile sauce, 83

Squash and zucchini, for roasted grouper with sesame-almond crust, 102

Summer fruit, for chilled fruit soup, 22

Summer shell bean minestre with tomato bruschetta, 2–3

Swordfish, grilled with Argentinian-style vegetable compote, 77

Syrup, for chilled fruit soup, 22

Syrup, for tropical fruit fandango, 109

T

Tiramisu, 69–70

Tomato bruschetta, with summer shell bean minestre, 5

Tomato coulis, with roasted egg plant cannelloni, 75

Tomato layer, for herbed eggplant, potato, and tomato torte, 83

Tomatoes, marinated with field peas vinaigrette, 4

Tropical fruit fandango, 108–109

Truffled macaroni, with medallions of lobster, baby green peas, 16

Tuna caper dressing, for morel crusted veal carpaccio with warm flaked tuna, 50

Tuna loin, grilled, in a stew of roasted peppers and lentils, fennel gratine, 53

Tuna, yellowfin, marinated and mustard-glazed, with red onion-cucumber salad, 61

V

Veal rib chop, pumpkin seed-crusted and pan roasted over potato and lobster mash with roasted corn jus, 108

Vegetable chips, with caramelized root vegetables and coq au vin, 77

Vegetable, mirepoix, with crisp taro-crusted 'opakapaka and grilled leek-fennel compote, 82

Vegetable, stock, for marinated portobello mushrooms stuffed with vegetarian paella, 106

Vegetable, stock, for summer shell bean minestre with tomato bruschetta, 4

Vegetable, sautéed, with curried salmon, 113

Vegetable, grilled, in a sandwich with new potato salad, 60

Vegetable, sautéed, with coq au vin, 76–77

Vegetable, sautéed, with pan-seared Pacific salmon in a wasabi-ginger crust, 86–87

Vegetarian paella, with grilled marinated portobello mushrooms, 107

Verbena ice cream, for ginger-snap cannoli, 31

Vidalia onion, stuffed with pork, 100

Vinaigrette for peas, with marinated red and yellow tomatoes, 4

Vinaigrette, for braised calamari and herb salad, 112

Vinaigrette, for glazed chicken breast with mesclun and daikon radish, 36–37

Vinaigrette, for spicy grilled shrimp, grit cakes, and country ham, 6

W

Warm banana-chocolate bread pudding with caramel sauce, kona coffee ice cream, and berries, 87–88

Warm flourless chocolate tart, white chocolate ice cream, and fresh mint sabayon, 53–54

Warm winter fruit compote of quince, prunes, and apricots soaked in Earl Grey Tea and oranges, 38–39

Wasabi-ginger crust, for pan-seared pacific salmon with ama ebi, leek creamed potatoes, and a maui onion jus, 86

White chocolate ice cream, with warm flourless chocolate tart and fresh mint sabayon, 54

Wild berry puree, for "pride of La Jolla" honey golden nest of summer sorbet trio, 47

Y

Yukon gold potatoes, with herbed, roasted breast of free range chicken, 85